Instant Pot
Cookbook
for Beginners

1000
Day Quick and Easy Instant Pot Recipes Meal Plan

The Most Complete Instant Pot Recipe Cookbook for Beginners

Katie Banks

INSTANT POT COOKBOOK FOR BEGINNERS
1000 DAY QUICK AND EASY INSTANT POT RECIPES M

D1514273

Copyright 2018 by World Good Foods Ltd   ISBN: 978-1-9993670-0-8
www.worldgoodfoods.com

Table of Contents

An Instant Pot Cookbook for Beginners

Have you just bought your new Instant Pot and you do not even know how to start? Maybe you have tried a few recipes, but you feel you cannot anything, completely right?

Are you on the other hand a more experienced user tired of complicated and time-consuming recipes, and would like to try something simpler, quicker and more straight to the point?

Either way, you got the right book. Here you will find first a guide on how to set up you Instant Pot from scratch. After this, you will be explained the basic water test necessary to make sure your device works correctly from the very beginning.

Knowing how and when to release the pressure in your Instant Pot is a key point to successfully cook your dishes. Use the wrong setting, or the right one for too short or too long, and you may spoil a nice recipe. For this reason, I have included a guide on pressure release options, so you always get your dishes cooked at their best.

Equally important is to have an effective cleaning routine, this will allow your Instant Pot to maintain all its cooking capabilities intact for the longest time possible. For you to achieve this, the important cleaning steps have been listed in this cookbook, so your pot is kept new and shiny.

Before moving onto the recipes, you will find an Instant Pot Button guide, so you fully understand what is going to happen and why every time you follow the detailed steps in the preparation section for all the meals included.

At the back of the book, a list of meal plans covering 1000 days of Instant Pot meal cooking has been included, so you never get tired of cooking or run out of ideas on how to create an eating schedule that is diverse, fun and most importantly delicious.

So now is time to seat, lean back and start browsing this complete cookbook, and once you know what to cook and when, get your Instant Pot, and start cooking!

Beginner's Guide for First-time Instant Pot Users

Who doesn't love a multi-function Instant Pot that cuts down by 70% the cooking time? You can prepare everything and anything in an Instant Pot, it is not messy and supports an eco-friendly and active lifestyle. It is a relatively new technology, so the way it works and how to make a large meal using the cooker can be a little confusing.

Your worries end here because we have an in-detail beginner's guide that will teach you everything from setting up the Instant Pot to cleaning it.

Let's get started:

SET UP THE INSTANT POT

Every Instant Pot package comes with a few accessories that will assist you at having a better understanding of how it works. When you open the box, make sure you find all these things inside it.

1. Manual
2. Quick reference guide
3. Steamer rack
4. Condensation collector
5. Recipe book
6. Soup scoop
7. Rice measuring cup
8. Rice paddle

All the information you need to set up the instant is mentioned in the manual and quick reference guide so go through it properly. If the Instant Pot isn't already assembled when arrives at your doorstep, you will have to install it. You have to install three things, which are inner pot, silicone sealing ring, and the lid.

1. Wash all of them thoroughly with warm water and clean them dry with a dry cloth.
2. Unwrap the Instant Pot and clean it with a warm wet cloth followed by a dry cloth.
3. Insert the stainless-steel inner pot and adjust it as directed in the manual.
4. Insert the silicone sealing ring. It should be fixed correctly, or else the pot won't get pressurized.
5. If you want to test the Instant Pot, add some water to it and hit boil. Make sure you cover it with a lid.

Opening and closing the lid is a little difficult so practice it a few times to get the hang of it. Different Instant Pots come with different instructions and symbols.

Open the instruction manual and learn how to use these different symbols. Ensure to clean the anti-block shield, the float valve, and the steam release valve every time before you cook because if any of them are obstructed, the pot will not switch on or the food will cook unevenly.

Instant Pot Water Test

After you are done learning how to assemble and operate the Instant Pot, it is time to put it through a water test. It is the easiest test to detect if the pot has any problems. Here's how you can perform the test:

1. Plug the Instant Pot to an electricity source and switch on the button.
2. Insert the inner pot and pour three cups or two glasses of water.
3. Check if the silicone sealing ring is inserted properly. If the insertion is correct, the ring will not move freely.
4. Seal the Instant Pot with the lid. The pop will beep three times to inform you that the lid is sealed in place.
5. Select Sealing open on the steam release handle.
6. Hit Steam and set the timer using the +/- symbol to set it to two minutes. Press Start.
7. If the pot is leaving a lot of steam, switch it off and remove the ring. Attach it again.
8. When the pot gets pressurized, a countdown will begin.

Once the timer is off, the pot will beep. In two minutes, the water should be boiling. If you can see bubbles, it means that the Instant Pot doesn't have any defects.

Pressure release options

Before you open the Instant Pot, you need to release the pressure. You have two pressure release options, which include - Natural Pressure Release (NPR) and Quick Pressure Release (QPR).

If you choose the Quick Pressure Release option, you will have to turn the venting knob to venting position as soon as the whistle goes off. Then, you will have to wait until the Floating Valve completely drops to open the pot. It is a faster option and prevents overcooking.

On the other hand, in Natural Pressure Release you have to wait untitl the Floating Valve drops. Then, you have to check if all pressure from inside the pot is released. It is a great alternative when you cook meat or rice because the latent helps in better cooking.

Here's a thumb rule you should remember:

1. **Natural release**

   Natural Pressure Release works well for legumes, rice, dried beans, meat and poultry, and liquid foods.

2. **Quick release**

   Always use Quick Pressure Release option for cooking eggs, stews, and vegetables. You can also it to cook fish since it the meat is delicate and can easily get overcooked.

Instant Pot Cleaning Routine

If you want the food to look and taste delicious, you need to clean it thoroughly after every cooking session. To ensure a deep clean, you need to follow this routine:

1. Remove the sealing ring and give it a quick rinse before you put it in the dishwasher. You can also steam it, but that's not necessary.
2. Take off the lid and the inner pot. Wipe all the stains on the inner pot with a wet warm cloth. Make sure you clean the cracks properly using a utensil cleaner brush.
3. Use warm soapy water to clean the lid.
4. Unassemble the float valve, the steam-release handle, and the anti-block shield and immerse them in soapy water as well.
5. Wash the steam rack under running water. You can use vinegar and water mix to retain the original color.
6. Wipe all parts dry and assemble the Instant Pot. Store it in a cool and dry place when not in use.

Instant Pot buttons Guide

There are a lot of buttons on the Instant Pot but you only need to use eight of them.

1. Manual/ pressure - to adjust time and pressure to cook food.
2. Sauté - to cook in a de-pressurized environment when you have to make large batches of food.
3. Rice - it is an automatic setting that cooks rice just the way you like it.
4. Slow cook button - to turn the Instant Pot into a slow cooker for hearty meals.
5. Steam - to quickly steam veggies and add it to the recipe.
6. Soup - this function doesn't let the liquid temperature get too high but cooks food thoroughly.
7. Timer - to adjust cooking time.
8. Keep Warm / Cancel - to warm the food before serving it or cancel the cooking.

Learning the Sauté Function

You can use the Instant Pot to sauté food just like you do in a skillet. Add some oil to the inner pot and add your mix of veggies and/or meat. Stir it using a rice paddle. You can adjust the temperature. Everything else remains the same.

Deciding the Amount of Liquid

The Instant Pot works a little differently than a usual saucepan or deep pan. Never fill water to the maximum limit line because the food will turn into a mush. If you add two cups of water to a recipe when you cook on the stove, then decrease the quantity to only one cup while cooking in an Instant Pot.

Eliminating Odors & Ensuring Food Safety

You need to clean the Instant Pot thoroughly to eliminate food odor and any leftover products so that the next batch of food doesn't get spoilt. You can dip the sealing ring in a mixture of water and vinegar. Add ¼ cup of vinegar to one cup of plain water. Always use warm water so that the stains and crumbs get removed easily.

BENEFITS OF PRESSURE COOKING

1. Retains nutrition

The longer you cook food, the more nutrients you lose. But when you use an Instant Pot, you reduce the cooking time by 70 percent. The food retains more B complex and C vitamin, which is lost when you cook for longer periods.

2. Kills pathogens

In an Instant Pot, food is cooked at a lower temperature and in an increased pressure environment. It helps to kill bacteria and other types of microorganisms that might be present in the food and is harmful to humans. The water of these microorganisms turn into vapor and cause a blast, which makes their pathogenic effect inactive.

CONVERTING RECIPES TO THE INSTANT POT

Quantity

First, you need to keep in mind the quantity you are cooking. Since these pots are smaller than other vessels you used to cook, measure properly. Don't fill it more than 2/3rd of the total volume.

Dairy products

If the recipe involves milk of any kind or dairy products, add it to a de-pressurized environment. If you add it to a pressurized environment, the food might blast when you open the pot. Wait till the very end to add dairy products.

Water

Add water mindfully. You don't want to add too much water or broth because the food will turn into a mush. Before you add food, add a cup of water to the pot to create steam, which speeds up the cooking process. If you think the dish doesn't need any more water, then don't put more.

3. Cooks food in less time

If you are too tired to cook, put the ingredients in the Instant Pot and the food is done in a short time. It comes very handy when you want to make big batches of food when you have guests coming over or for meal planning. Also, while the food is getting cooked, you don't need to stir it as the pot is completely sealed. It makes multitasking easy as you can get over work done during the cooking time.

4. Less cleaning

There are no residues on the countertop or on the stove. No oil spilled on the walls and floors as well. A little amount of water escapes the Instant Pot but it rarely drips down. When you are washing the pot, you can clean the water easily. You can also serve food directly in the pot, so you can save the cleaning of one serving bowl as well.

5. Preserving food

While big Instant Pots are used to make food, the small can be used to make pickles, jams, and jellies. You can start by cooking the food in the pot along with sugar or brine solution. If you want the food to have less water in the end, you have to add less water. Once it is thoroughly cooked, you can transfer it to a saucepan and cook until you achieve the desired consistency.

Cooking time

If you are worried about the cooking time, here's a trick that will help you. Note one ingredient from your list that takes the longest to cook. Check the number of minutes that particular food item takes to cook in an Instant Pot. Viola! You have got your cooking time.

On an average, chicken takes six to eight minutes, beef takes 15 to 20 minutes, dried black beans take 20 to 25 minutes, and brown rice takes 22 to 25 minutes. Veggies take around three to four minutes only. You can also cook the recipe in two phases. If you are making chicken cauliflower soup, cook the chicken first as it takes up to 15 minutes. Take it out and then cook the cauliflower for three minutes. Add the remaining ingredients and cook it for another five minutes.

Instant Pot does come with some limitations. You can't cook meat served rare or foods that need a crispy brown outer layer in the pot.

Chicken

Spicy Roasted Chicken

Serving: 4

Cooking Time: 30 min

The spicy roasted chicken is going to be a feast for your senses. We have cooked it succulently garlic, pepper and red wine. The chicken is slow cooked to make it more tender and delicious. We have also added an assortment of vegetables like eggplants, pumpkin, tomatoes and capsicum. The soy sauce and oregano enrich the flavor and makes the sauce delicious. It's a complete meal you can serve to guests and family for some praise!

NUTRITIONAL VALUES

Calories 925 kcal

Fat 63 g

Total Carbs 78 g

Protein 87 g

INGREDIENTS

6 tbsp olive oil

1 full chicken breast

1 medium-sized onion. Sliced

8 garlic cloves, minced

2 eggplants, cut in cubes

1 capsicum, diced

12 oz Pumpkin, cut into cubes

1 green pepper, diced

4 tomatoes, steam, grinded

1 cup dry red wine

4 tablespoons soy sauce

4 cups chicken broth

3 teaspoons oregano, dried

DIRECTIONS:

1. Set pot to sauté.

2. Heat olive oil. Add chicken breasts and sear until brown. Remove and set aside.

3. Add onions and garlic. Cook until garlic turns brown.

4. Add eggplant, capsicum and pumpkin. Stir well and add in peppers. Stir in pureed tomatoes.

5. Add wine, soy sauce, and chicken broth.

6. Add the chicken.

7. Put some salt, pepper, and oregano.

8. Pour in the broth.

9. Secure lid and cook on high for 10 min.

10. Apply a natural release.

11. Serve hot sided with bread.

COOKING TIPS

Some fresh vegetables will be a fantastic idea with the spicy chicken roast. Throw in some cucumber and red onion salad to complement the spicy sauce while you enjoy it with some bread. You can also add some chili flakes to the sauce to give it a kick - yummy!

Hainanese Chicken

Serving: 3

Cooking time: 4 hours

We have got something from the shores of China- presenting Hainanese Chicken! The secret to the oriental taste is the Pandan leaves which are used extensively in South East Asian and South Asia as a flavoring agent. The chicken is slow cooked for hours absorbing all the flavors and turning into a succulent delight. Even though it takes a long time to prepare, the steps are pretty simple. Enjoy it with a delicious ginger dip.

NUTRITIONAL VALUES

Calories 435 kcal

Fat 15 g

Total Carbs 9 g

Protein 65g

INGREDIENTS

1 Whole Chicken

1 oz ginger

5 cloves Garlic, crushed

4 pieces Pandan Leaves/ cilantro bundled

1 tsp. Salt

1 tbsp. Sesame Oil

For Ginger Dip:

2 tbsp. Ginger

1 tsp. Garlic

1 tbsp. Chicken/ vegetable Stock

1 tsp. Sesame Oil

1 tsp. Sugar

Salt, to taste

DIRECTIONS:

1. Mix chicken, ginger, garlic, leaves, and salt in the instant pot.

2. Add water to submerge completely the chicken and cook on slow cooker to low for 4 hours.

3. Remove chicken from the pot and cool using an ice bath for 15 minutes.

4. While you do the previous step, combine all ingredients for the ginger dip in a food processor and make a coarse paste.

5. Remove chicken from the bath, drain, and chop into pieces. Put onto a serving platter and brush it with sesame oil.

6. Serve with ginger dip by the side.

COOKING TIPS

The best way to serve this recipe is with a plate of white rice- that's how the Hainanese people eat it. You can also have it with a chili dip. Just put together lime, salt, ginger, garlic, sriracha, sugar and two tablespoons of chicken broth. Just blend in a food processor and you are ready!

Lemongrass Braised Chicken

We have used chicken thighs for our lemongrass braised chicken as they are best for this way of cooking. They end up producing so much flavor while being one of the inexpensive cuts. You can cook the thighs for a large number of people, and this simple recipe is a delicious way to prepare them. We have added the fresh lemongrass flavor which infuses with tomatoes, banana peppers and fish sauce for a great taste.

NUTRITIONAL VALUES

Calories 1025 kcal   Total Carbs 32 g

Fat 67 g   Protein 75g

INGREDIENTS

4 Chicken Thighs, bone-in

1 stalk Lemongrass, bruised and bundled-up

2 tablespoons Tamarind Paste

1 thumb-sized piece Fresh Turmeric, cut into thin strips

2 cups Chicken Stock

2 Roma Tomatoes, quartered

2 Shallots, quartered

2 Banana Peppers

1 Radish, peeled and chopped into 2" batons

Mustard Leaves

Salt or Fish Sauce to taste

DIRECTIONS:

1. Combine all ingredients inside pot.

2. Cook on slow cooker mode set low for 4 1/2 hours. Release pressure naturally.

3. Add mustard leaves and leave it wilt for a few minutes over a warm surface.

COOKING TIPS

You can garnish the chicken with some finely chopped cilantro for a great taste. Ginger can be a good addition if you enjoy the flavor. If you want the recipe a bit spicy, you can chop a little onion and garlic and put it with all the other ingredients in the pot.

Creamy Italian Chicken

Serving: 10 min

Cooking Time: 25 min

The creamy and smooth chicken dish can be prepared just within 15 minutes with an instant pot. The secret to the flavor of this dish is the Italian seasoning we will be using but you can skip it too. You can serve it with a plate of pasta or rice to make it more filling for your family and children. It is perfect for a quick lunch or dinner and requires only a few ingredients.

NUTRITIONAL VALUES

Calories 750 kcal

Fat 62 g

Total Carbs 7 g

Protein 48 g

INGREDIENTS

1.5lb chicken breast

1 cup cream cheese cream

1 cup chicken stock

1/2 cup heavy cream

5 tablespoon butter

1 head broccoli, approximately ½ kg

1-1/2 tablespoon Italian seasoning (optional)

DIRECTIONS:

1. Preheat the pot on sauté mode.

2. Cut broccoli into florets.

3. Heat butter until shimmering.

4. Add chicken and fry until golden brown, for about 5 minutes.

5. Add heavy cream, broccoli and Italian seasoning.

6. Secure the lid and change to manual mode.

7. Cook on high for 10 minutes.

8. Do a quick pressure release and unlock the lid.

9. Add cream cheese, mix well and remove.

COOKING TIPS

This rich and creamy dish is open for experimenting. You can try putting different types of veggies like peas and corn. It will also taste delicious with some mushrooms and you can throw in a handful of baby spinach in the last 10 minutes of preparation. You can also use low-fat cream if you are watching your weight.

Rotisserie Chicken

You may find it tempting to just get readymade rotisserie from the store, but we are going to give you a homemade version that is far better. The chicken turns out moist and crispy on the outside with delicate flavor of the herbs we will be using. It is simple to make and requires no messy steps. You can serve it as the main dish with a siding of French fries or coleslaw if you like.

NUTRITIONAL VALUES

Calories 720 kcal   Total Carbs 5 g

Fat 60 g   Protein 40g

INGREDIENTS

1.5-2lb whole chicken

½ cup butter

½ lb cream cheese

1 cup chicken broth

1 tablespoon paprika

Salt and pepper to taste

For serving:

Fresh parsley

Lemon

DIRECTIONS:

1. Rinse chicken and suck the excess moisture with paper towel.

2. In a large mixing bowl, mix well butter and cream cheese together.

3. Add paprika, oregano, salt and pepper, mix until well combined.

4. With the help of a sharp knife, poke the slits in the back of chicken.

5. Generously rub the butter and spice mixture onto each side of the chicken.

6. Place the chicken into the pot, add in the chicken broth, cover and cook for 30 minutes on high.

7. Once the chicken is done, release the pressure naturally.

8. Transfer the chicken to a serving dish.

9. Garnish with fresh parsley and serve with lemon.

COOKING TIPS

You may also use some rosemary along with the parsley to enhance the flavor of the dish. If you don't want to use butter, you can try alternate it with some olive oil. You can use aluminum foil to store the chicken and retain the moistness for a long time.

Sweet & Sticky Chicken

Serving: 4

Cooking time: 35 minutes

This is going to leave a tangy feeling on your taste buds! The sweet and sticky chicken is saucy and thick and makes for a great appetizer. It's also got a lovely flavor with the garlic and parsley we are going to use. You can also eat it with some rice or veggies for a sumptuous lunch or dinner. Be sure to make some extra as your hubby and kids are sure to ask for more!

NUTRITIONAL VALUES

Calories 365 kcal

Fat 30 g

Total Carbs 3 g

Protein 19 g

INGREDIENTS

1lb chicken thigh

1/3 cup of honey

1/3 cup of water

1 cup tomato, chopped

3 clove garlic, minced

4 tablespoon butter

1 package stevia

Salt and pepper to taste

For serving:

Fresh parsley

Lime wedges

DIRECTIONS:

1. Season chicken thighs with salt and pepper.

2. Set to sauté mode.

3. Add butter and chicken thighs, cook for 4 minutes until golden.

4. Add garlic and tomatoes, cook stirring constantly for 1 minute. Add water and honey.

5. Put lid on and set valve to sealing position.

6. Cook on meat mode for 30 minutes.

7. After the time is up, let the pressure release naturally.

8. Open the lid and dish out the ingredients.

9. Garnish with some fresh parsley and serve with lime wedges.

COOKING TIPS

We have used stevia for as an alternate for sugar in this dish. You can also use sugar if you don't have any problem consuming it. If you want, you may also add some broccoli to the dish. Add the broccoli florets while you are cooking the chicken on sauté mode.

Worcestershire Chicken Salad

Salads are great for a healthy meal anytime of the day. The chicken salad will use Worcestershire which is a delicious ingredient made from fermented fish and variety of spices. It provides the unique taste to the recipe which can be prepared in around half an hour. The recipe is perfect for those following a keto diet and comes high fat content and medium protein. It is quite filling and will keep you satiated for hours.

NUTRITIONAL VALUES

Calories 420 kcal   Total Carbs 4 g

Fat 31 g   Protein 30 g

INGREDIENTS

1 lb chicken, boneless

1 head lettuce, chopped

1 tablespoon Worcestershire

1 cup cottage cheese

3 tablespoon olive oil

1 tablespoon lemon juice

Salt and pepper to taste

For extra serving:

1 cup baby tomatoes

DIRECTIONS:

1. Marinate the chicken with Worcestershire, lemon juice, black pepper and salt.

2. Heat oil to the instant pot and add marinated chicken. Fry on sauté mode until nice golden and crisp, add half cup of water.

3. Lock the lid into place, setting the valve to the sealing position.

4. Hit manual mode and cook on high for 30 minutes.

5. Once finished cooking, allow the pot to release pressure naturally.

6. Turn the valve to the venting position and carefully open the lid.

7. In a large mixing bowl place chopped lettuce, baby tomatoes and cottage cheese.

8. Top with crispy chicken and serve.

COOKING TIPS

We have use Worcestershire in the salad for the aroma and taste. But if you find it difficult to find Worcestershire there are a few substitutes you can try. You may replace the Worcestershire with soy sauce or oyster sauce. But do keep in mind nothing can entirely replace Worcestershire.

Chili Chicken Rice

Serving: 4
Cooking time: 20 minutes

Chili chicken is one of the most popular Chinese dishes out there. Today we are going to make a simple chili chicken with rice which can be prepared in a short time. It can make for a light meal or heavy meal depending on the amount of rice you are cooking. You only use minimal ingredients to get a wonderful flavor which tastes spicy and hot. Let's surprise your family today with some easy to cook oriental recipe.

NUTRITIONAL VALUES

Calories 450 kcal

Fat 6 g

Total Carbs 62 g

Protein 33 g

INGREDIENTS

1 lb chicken, cubed

1.5-2 cups rice

3 cups chicken broth

1/2 cup onion, sliced

1 teaspoon cumin

1 teaspoon chili powder

1 tablespoon oil

Salt to taste

For serving:

2 lemons sliced

Fresh parsley, chopped

DIRECTIONS:

1. Set sauté mode on the instant pot.

2. Heat oil until shimmering, add onion and sauté for 5 minutes.

3. Add chicken, cumin, chili powder, and salt; cook for additional 5 minutes.

4. Once the chicken is browned, add rice and mix well.

5. Now add in the chicken broth, cook stirring constantly for 1 minute, close the lid.

6. Set the pot to the manual mode.

7. Cook on high for 10 minutes.

8. After the time is up, apply a quick pressure release.

9. Unlock the lid, garnish with some lemon slices and fresh parsley.

COOKING TIPS

We have used a standard amount of chili in the dish. If you want to make it hotter, you can use ancho or chipotle chili powder. While serving you can also add other crispy toppings to make the dish taste heavenly. We recommend some shredded lettuce if you want some greens.

Cauliflower Chicken Rice

Serving: 4
Cooking time: 30 minutes

This nutritious and sumptuous cauliflower chicken rice is ideal for a great family dinner or lunch. It packs 480 calories with medium protein and fat content and perfect for the people of keto diet. The recipe tastes way better than the versions you get at takeaways and is a lot healthier. If your kids don't like cauliflower, this is the best way to make them eat the vegetable as they won't be able to make the difference.

NUTRITIONAL VALUES

Calories 480 kcal

Fat 39 g

Total Carbs 7 g

Protein 26 g

INGREDIENTS

1 lb chicken, cubed

4 cups cauliflower rice

1 cup of vegetable stock

1 cup heavy cream

1 teaspoon cumin

1 teaspoon chili flakes

3 tablespoon butter

Salt to taste

For serving:

2 lemons sliced

Fresh parsley, chopped

DIRECTIONS:

1. Using a food processor, process cauliflower florets until small rice-sized pieces.

2. Preheat the pot on sauté setting and heat butter.

3. Add chicken to the pot and sauté for 5 minutes until nice golden.

4. Add cauliflower rice, stock, cream, cumin, chili flakes and salt, mix all the ingredients until well combined.

5. Place the lid on and lock it.

6. Set the pot to the manual mode and cook for 30 minutes on high.

7. Once the instant pot timer , allow the pot to release pressure naturally.

8. Remove the lid and transfer the chicken cauliflower rice to a serving plate.

9. Top with some lemon and chopped parsley.

COOKING TIPS

You can experiment with different vegetables along with cauliflower in this recipe. Some carrots and beans can blend well along with the cauliflower rice. Make sure to cut the vegetables in small pieces before you add them to the mix. Add the vegetables after the chicken has turned golden in the pot.

Instant Carrot Chicken Pie

Serving: 4

Cooking time: 30 minutes

The instant carrot chicken pie is really easy to prepare and one of the easiest comfort food. It comes packed with chicken and carrots and topped with some mozzarella cheese and breadcrumbs. It packs high amounts of protein and can keep you going for hours through the day. You can have it for a filling breakfast and save a few slices for your lunch. We have also used some Italian seasoning to bring out the aroma and flavor.

NUTRITIONAL VALUES

Calories 425 kcal

Fat 17 g

Total Carbs 13 g

Protein 54 g

INGREDIENTS

2 lb chicken, cubed

2 cup chicken broth

2 large carrots, diced

1 cup corn kernels

1/2 cup cream

1 teaspoon onion powder

1 tablespoon Italian seasoning

For topping:

1 cup bread crumbs

1 cup mozzarella cheese

DIRECTIONS:

1. Turn Instant pot to manual mode.

2. Place all the ingredients except cream into the pot.

3. Cover and cook on high for 20 minutes.

4. Once time is up, apply a quick pressure release.

5. Carefully unlock the lid, stir in cream.

6. Preheat oven to 350F.

7. Transfer the chicken to a greased baking dish.

8. Top with bread crumbs and mozzarella cheese, bake for 10 minutes brown and golden.

9. Remove from the oven and serve warm.

COOKING TIPS

You can experiment with the choice of toppings on the pie. You can also use an aluminum foil to retain the moisture of the chicken and make the cleaning process easy. If you are on a diet or watching your weight you can use low fat version of the cream.

Creamy Chicken Pie

The crispy and crunchy chicken pie comes with an added dose of cream which gives it a blend of richness. It has the goodness of broccoli and chicken and makes a healthy dish for your hubby and children. It also serves a high content of protein and fat and can be ideal for those on keto diet. You can serve the crunchy chicken pie with some mashed potatoes to make a wholesome meal for your family.

NUTRITIONAL VALUES

Calories 700 kcal   Total Carbs 6 g

Fat 58 g   Protein 37 g

INGREDIENTS

2 lb chicken, cubed

1 cup broccoli, cut into florets

2 cups cheddar cheese, shredded

1 cup cream

1/2 cup of chicken broth

1 small onion, chopped

1 tablespoon Italian seasoning

Salt and black pepper to taste

For topping:

1 cup almond flour

1 cup mozzarella cheese

1 cup sour cream

DIRECTIONS:

1. Select manual mode.

2. Place chicken, broth, broccoli, cream, onion, Italian seasoning, black pepper and salt into the pot.

3. Secure the lid into and select manual to cook on high for 25 minutes.

4. Once finished cooking, turn the valve to the venting position and carefully open the lid.

5. Meanwhile preheat the oven to 350F.

6. Now transfer the chicken to a baking dish coated with cooking spray.

7. Top with almond flour and mozzarella cheese.

8. Place the dish into the oven and bake for 10 minutes until the top is nice golden and crisp.

9. Serve with sour cream.

COOKING TIPS

You can use aluminum foil to make the baking and cleaning process easy. The dish can also accommodate some veggies if you want to make it more filling- put in some carrots or peas. You may also add in other forms of meat like some crispy bacon and make this recipe a winner!

Turkey

Portobello Turkey Legs

Portobello mushrooms have quite a few health benefits. They come with natural anti-inflammatory properties and antioxidants and can be an ideal substitute for meat. You also get a good dose of B vitamins along with selenium and copper. They are also low on carbs and contain some fiber. We have combined Portobello mushrooms with juicy and tender turkey legs along with some crispy bacon. The chosen herbs and spices come together for a sumptuous dish!

NUTRITIONAL VALUES

Calories 700 kcal

Fat 36 g

Total Carbs 3 g

Protein 83 g

INGREDIENTS

- 4 turkey legs
- Sea salt and black pepper to taste
- 3 tbsp. olive oil
- 2 rashers smoked bacon, chopped
- 1 medium red onion, diced
- 1 large carrot, peeled and diced
- 1 stalk celery, diced
- 1 cup Portobello mushrooms, diced
- 4 cloves garlic, minced
- 2 tbsp. sweet sherry wine
- 1 tsp. sherry vinegar
- 2 tsp. Worcestershire/ soy sauce
- 1 1/2 cup chicken stock
- ½ tsp. dried rosemary
- ½ tsp. dried thyme
- 4 bay leaves

DIRECTIONS:

1. Season turkey legs with salt and pepper.

2. Set to Sauté and add oil. When it is hot sauté the chicken legs until golden all over. Remove and set aside in a bowl.

3. Set to Sauté and add the bacon, onions, carrot, celery and mushrooms and sauté for 5 minutes until the onions are soft. Add garlic and sauté for another minute.

4. Drop sherry and vinegar and cook for a couple of minutes before adding the stock and Worcestershire sauce. Stir to remove burnt bits from the bottom of the pan.

5. Add herbs and season with salt and pepper to taste. Add the legs and any remaining juice. Set to manual (high) for 20 minutes. When done allow the pressure to go naturally for 10 minutes before releasing the remaining pressure manually.

6. Season with salt and pepper.

COOKING TIPS

You can check the tenderness of the turkey legs to ensure you have cooked them the right way. You should be able to pull off the meat from the bone using a serving spoon. Serve the dish along with some boiled peas and spoonful of mashed potato on the side.

Balsamic Turkey Meatballs

Serving: 2

Cooking time: 10 minutes

Meatballs are one of the most popular appetizers as they are seasoned balls of meat covered in savory sauce. The recipe uses seasoned ground turkey presented in a simple sauce made from balsamic vinegar and blueberries. The balsamic vinegar provides the right amount of tanginess while the blueberries give the sauce a natural sweetness. It is also easy to prepare and comes together in just 10 minutes of cooking. You will need to prepare the blueberry sauce first.

NUTRITIONAL VALUES

Calories 705 kcal

Fat 35 g

Total Carbs 4 g

Protein 55 g

INGREDIENTS

1 lb. ground turkey

1 small onion, finely chopped

2 cloves garlic, minced

2 tsp. Worcestershire/soy sauce

3 tbsp. panko bread crumbs

1 egg, beaten

¼ tsp. freshly ground black pepper, or to taste

3 tbsp. parmesan cheese, finely grated

1 tsp. Italian herb seasoning

For Blueberry Sauce:

8 oz. blueberries (plus 2 tbsp. for garnish)

1/2 cup white sugar

½ tsp kosher sea salt

½ tsp. black pepper

3 sprigs fresh rosemary

3 sprig fresh thyme

1 tsp. balsamic vinegar

DIRECTIONS:

1. Use a processor to blend the ingredients of the sauce, add the mix into the pot along with ½ cup of water. Mix it well stirring and cook on high for 5 minutes followed by applying a quick release, and remove the lid.

2. Add all the meatball ingredients to a bowl and mix well. Turn the mixture into 1-inch sized meatballs.

3. Drop meatballs into the pot making sure they are all covered by sauce. Set to Manual (High) for 5 minutes. When done apply a quick pressure release.

4. Present garnished by scattering some blueberries.

COOKING TIPS

The blueberry sauce we made for the turkey can be used with different kinds of protein or meat. You can consider it as an all-purpose barbecue sauce. Any time you think of using a sweet and tangy barbecue sauce, this blueberry sauce can be your best alternative. Give it a try!

American Barbecue Turkey

Serving: 4

Cooking time: 35 minutes

Here's a turkey recipe which is easy to make and can be prepared within 35 minutes. You will just love the creamy taste of the turkey and mushrooms thanks to the cream cheese and heavy cream we are using. The recipe packs high amounts of energy and gives your daily requirement of protein and fat. Surprise your family with the delicious recipe cooked in American style for a rich taste. Try it out today for dinner!

NUTRITIONAL VALUES

Calories 750 kcal   Total Carbs 9 g

Fat 64 g   Protein 36 g

INGREDIENTS

1 lb. turkey breast

1/2 cup of chicken broth

1 cup heavy cream

2 cups cream cheese

1 cup mushrooms

1/2 cup Keto or Low sugar barbecue sauce

DIRECTIONS:

1. Place the turkey into the pot.

2. Add chicken broth and BBQ sauce, cover and cook on manual mode for 25 minutes.

3. Once the cooking time is over, release pressure naturally.

4. Now add in the heavy cream, cream cheese and mushrooms.

5. Cover and cook on sauté mode for 10 minutes.

6. Transfer the creamy turkey and mushrooms to a plate and serve.

COOKING TIPS

We have used a keto version or low sugar barbecue sauce while preparing the dish. If you are not that health conscious, you can go for normal barbecue sauce too. You can garnish the dish with some cilantro and pepper if you want to add a tinge of hotness to it.

Turkey Meatballs

Serving: 4

Cooking time: 25 minutes

Turkey meatballs make a healthy option as they are leaner than beef. It comes with high amount of protein and provides a number of minerals and vitamins such as potassium, iron, zinc and vitamin B6. The recipe is loaded with flavor and the meatballs stay incredibly moist on the inside which just seem to melt in your mouth. The Italian seasoning brings out the aroma and flavor which you are going to fall in love with!

NUTRITIONAL VALUES

Calories 474 kcal

Fat 38.66 g

Total Carbs 8 g

Protein 26 g

INGREDIENTS

1lb ground turkey

1/2 cup onion, chopped

1 cup ground almond or flour

1 medium egg

5 oz olive oil

1 tablespoon Italian seasoning

DIRECTIONS:

1. Mix all the ingredients in a food processor except onion and oil. Mix until well combined.

2. Transfer the mix to a bowl, then add chopped onion.

3. Using your hands, work the mixture together; mix until all the ingredients are well combined.

4. Roll the mixture into 15 meatballs, cover and refrigerate for 10 minutes.

5. Turn on the instant pot and add oil, heat until shimmering.

6. Add meatballs and fry until evenly browned, about 5 minutes.

7. Set the instant pot to the manual mode (high), cover and cook for 20 minutes.

8. Once the pot beeps, remove the lid and transfer the meatball onto a serving plate.

9. Insert skewer into each balls and serve.

COOKING TIPS

You can prepare a batch of meatballs and save them for eating throughout the day. They can be refrigerated easily and reheated in very less time. You can also try preparing a sauce to go along with the meatballs. We leave it on you to decide what type of sauce you want to make!

Sausage & Veggie Muffins

How about some muffins made with the goodness of turkey and veggies?

That's what we are going to make today! The muffins can be the perfect breakfast giving you the energy to remain active throughout the day. You can make them in advance and keep them ready whenever you have the hunger pangs. The bell pepper and oregano provide the flavor and aroma that will make anyone drool. It can be prepared in 15 minutes and can be a saver when guests come knocking on your door.

NUTRITIONAL VALUES

Calories 350 kcal   Total Carbs 7 g

Fat 22 g   Protein 29 g

INGREDIENTS

8 eggs

1/2lb. turkey sausages, sliced

1-1/2 cup cheddar cheese

1 cup milk

1 large bell pepper, chopped

1 cup spinach, finely chopped

1 teaspoon oregano

Salt and black pepper

DIRECTIONS:

1. Grease 4 ovenproof cups with some butter.

2. In a large mixing bowl, whisk eggs, cheese, milk, oregano, black pepper and salt.

3. Mix in sausages, spinach and bell pepper.

4. Carefully fill each cup with 2/3 of the mixture.

5. Add 2 cups of water to the Instant pot and place a trivet.

6. Cover the cups with foil and place it on the trivet.

7. Secure the lid and cook on manual mode (high) for 15 minutes.

8. Once the muffins are done, do a quick pressure release.

9. Remove the muffins from the instant pot.

10. Serve warm with your favorite sauce.

COOKING TIPS

We have used bell pepper and chopped spinach in our recipe as they are easily available all around the year. But you are free to change the veggies according to the seasonal availability. That way you get a different feeling and taste while keeping the turkey consistent in your recipe.

Turkey with Spinach and Mushrooms

Serving: 4
Cooking time: 30 minutes

We bring the health benefits of turkey combined with mushroom and spinach in this recipe. It packs 400 calories and can give you a energy boost whenever you require it. It is quite filling and can be served for breakfast or lunch with a plate of pasta or rice. You can prepare the dish well within 30 minutes using a limited number of ingredients. It is great on taste and nice to be enjoyed with some company.

NUTRITIONAL VALUES

Calories 400 kcal | Total Carbs 3 g

Fat 19 g | Protein 55 g

INGREDIENTS

2lb. turkey meat

1 cup chicken broth

1/2 cup cream

1 cup mushrooms, sliced

1 cup spinach, chopped

1 teaspoon garlic powder

1 tablespoon olive oil

Salt and pepper to taste

For garnishing:

Fresh cilantro leaves, chopped

COOKING TIPS

Like many other dishes, you can also experiment a bit on your own. You can add in your choice of vegetables in the recipe to complement the taste and flavor. You can also prepare a separate vegetable dish and have it along with this recipe for a complete lunch or dinner.

DIRECTIONS:

1. Turn the Instant pot on sauté mode.

2. Heat oil and add turkey, cook until nice brown; for about 10 minutes.

3. Once the turkey is browned add garlic powder, salt and pepper, mix until well combined.

4. Now add in the spinach, mushrooms and broth.

5. Secure the lid into place and set the valve to sealing position.

6. Select manual mode and cook on high for 20 minutes.

7. Once cooking time is up, apply a quick pressure release.

8. Carefully open the lid and stir in the cream.

9. Transfer the turkey to a serving dish.

10. Garnish with some fresh cilantro leaves.

Cheesy Turkey with Mushrooms

This recipe gives you a strong dose of energy coming with 730 calories. You don't need to fret about the 62g of fat as it comes from turkey which is far leaner than beef and other meat. Your kids and family will love the creamy richness of the dish while they get to enjoy the health benefits of spinach and mushrooms. Prepare the dish in advance as there is quite a few steps to carry out.

NUTRITIONAL VALUES

Calories 730 kcal

Fat 62 g

Total Carbs 5 g

Protein 37 g

INGREDIENTS

2 lb turkey meat

1 cup chicken broth

1 cup cream cheese

1 cup mushrooms, sliced

1 cup spinach, chopped

3 clove garlic, minced

1 tablespoon butter

Salt and pepper to taste

For garnishing:

Fresh cilantro leaves, chopped

DIRECTIONS:

1. Turn the Instant pot on sauté mode.

2. Heat butter until shimmering, add garlic and fry for 5 minutes.

3. Add turkey and cook until golden brown; for about 10 minutes.

4. Once the turkey is browned add spinach and mushrooms, cook for additional 5 minutes.

5. Now add in the broth.

6. Season with some salt and black pepper.

7. Lock the lid and select manual mode to cook on high for 20 minutes.

8. Once finished cooking, allow the pot to release pressure naturally.

9. Turn the valve to the venting position and carefully open the lid.

10. Add cream cheese, mix until well combined.

11. Transfer the turkey to a serving dish and garnish with some fresh cilantro leaves.

COOKING TIPS

You are free to add a side dish to the recipe if you want. A siding of rice or tortillas will be great with this creamy chicken with mushrooms making it wholesome. If you have leftover, you can freeze it and reheat quickly whenever you want to grab a bite.

Pork

Pork Roast in Honey and Garlic

Serving: 3
Cooking time: 20 minutes

Pork shoulder is a versatile and tasty cut of meat which is also inexpensive. It is perfect for slow cooking, and that's why we have chosen it. You will need boneless pork shoulder roast which will be cooked in honey, chili garlic sauce and chicken broth till it is tender and juicy. We have also put in some baked beans and mushrooms to complement the taste of honey and garlic. You can get the dish ready for dinner in just 20 minutes.

NUTRITIONAL VALUES

Calories 780 kcal   Total Carbs 47 g

Fat 25 g   Protein 92 g

INGREDIENTS

2 lb. boneless pork shoulder roast

3 tablespoons honey

3 tablespoons sesame seeds

3 tablespoons chili garlic sauce

Salt and black pepper, as per taste

1 can baked beans

1 cup sun dried tomatoes

9 cloves garlic, finely chopped

1 medium onion, diced

9 button mushrooms, sliced

1 cup chicken broth

2 tablespoons sour cream

DIRECTIONS:

1. Wash and dry the roast. Use a mixing bowl to combine honey, sesame seeds, chili garlic sauce with some salt and pepper. Rub the mixture over the pork. Place the pork in the fridge for 25 minutes.

2. Pour some olive oil into the pot and place the pork in.

3. Add baked beans, tomatoes, garlic, onions, and mushrooms. Drop some chicken broth along with cream and stir every well.

4. Add salt and pepper.

5. Seal the lid and cook for 25 minutes on high pressure.

6. Apply a natural pressure release.

COOKING TIPS

You can increase the amount of the garlic to make the recipe more spicy. If you want the sauce to be a bit thicker, you can add 2/3 cup of parmesan cheese which really blends well with the honey and garlic. The leftover sauce can also make some great stir fry sauce.

Popeye Frittata

Serving: 4

Cooking time: 25 minutes

You can get strong and fit like Popeye with our Popeye Frittata. We have used 1 lb of spinach which comes loaded with vitamin B2, vitamin C, vitamin A and vitamin K. It is also a good source of iron, magnesium and manganese. We will be using chorizo in these easy to make frittatas which you can serve for breakfast or have as snacks anytime of the day. So, let's start getting the ingredients together!

NUTRITIONAL VALUES

Calories 660 kcal

Fat 556 g

Total Carbs 8 g

Protein 33 g

INGREDIENTS

1lb. fresh spinach, chopped

8 eggs

5 oz. chorizo

1 cup mozzarella cheese, shredded

4 tablespoon butter

1 cup heavy cream

Salt and pepper to taste

DIRECTIONS:

1. Heat butter in a fry pan and fry chorizo for about 5 minutes, once done set aside.

2. In a large mixing bowl, whisk eggs, cheese, cream, chorizo, salt and pepper.

3. Add chopped spinach and mix well.

4. Grease a 7-inch pan with some oil.

5. Pour the egg mixture into the pan and cover with foil.

6. Add a cup of water to the instant pot.

7. Now place the trivet into the pot and then the prepared pan over the trivet.

8. Lock the lid into the place and make sure the valve is in the sealing position.

9. Select manual and cook for 20 minutes (high).

10. Once the eggs are done, release the pressure naturally about 10 minutes.

11. Then quick release any remaining pressure and unlock the cover. Flip the valve to the venting position.

12. Carefully remove the pan from the pot, using a knife gently loosen the sides of frittata.

13. Invert the frittata onto a plate and serve.

COOKING TIPS

If you are watching your weight, you may want to replace the eggs with egg whites to get a low fat and high protein frittata. You can also add in some vegetables to make it more filling and serve the dish for lunch. Toast some bread and you have a perfect recipe for your dinner.

Bacon-Stuffed Avocados

Some of us can eat avocados for days at a stretch without getting sick of them. So we have thought of a quick and easy lunch idea with avocados stuffed with bacon. It is perfect for a meal or snack and is an healthy option with low amount of carb. The dish will be great for people who are on a weight loss diet with limited intake of carbs. It's easy to make and can be prepared in 20 minutes.

NUTRITIONAL VALUES

Calories 460 kcal

Fat 38 g

Total Carbs 13 g

Protein 20 g

INGREDIENTS

8 eggs

4 avocados

8 bacon strips, cooked and crumbled

1 teaspoon of chili flakes

Salt and black pepper to taste

For garnishing:

Fresh parsley, finely chopped

DIRECTIONS:

1. Cut the avocados in half lengthwise and remove pits.

2. Using a tablespoon, scoop out the flesh from each avocado.

3. Add bacon strips, chili flakes, black pepper and salt to the avocado flesh.

4. Mix until well combined.

5. Scoop the mixture back to the avocado cups.

6. Crack an egg into each avocado cup.

7. Pour 1 cup of water into the pot and place a trivet.

8. Lock the lid in place and set vent to the sealing position.

9. Select high pressure and set the time to 20 minutes.

10. When time is up apply a quick pressure release.

11. Flip the valve to the venting position and remove the lid.

12. Remove avocados from the pot.

13. Garnish with some fresh parsley and serve.

COOKING TIPS

You can prepare a batch of stuffed avocados and put them in the fridge. They can be reheated quickly and come handy when you start feeling hungry. You can also pack them for lunch and have a quick bite of healthy and high protein snack. You can also add some cilantro to your garnishing.

Japanese Balsamic Pork Roast

Serving: 4
Cooking time: 40 minutes

Japanese Balsamic pork roast is one of the popular dishes you can make for dinner. The dish looks like you have to spend a lot of time on it, but you can serve it on the table in just 40 minutes. We have used a portion of teriyaki sauce which gives the recipe its flavor and Japanese taste. It is great for people on keto diet as it comes with limited carbs and high content of fat.

NUTRITIONAL VALUES

Calories 535 kcal

Fat 45 g

Total Carbs 9 g

Protein 24 g

INGREDIENTS

1lb pork shoulder

3 cup chicken broth

1 cup heavy cream

½ cup teriyaki sauce

3 tablespoon butter

1 teaspoon salt and black pepper

For serving (optional):

Fresh parsley

Lime wedges

DIRECTIONS:

1. Combine teriyaki sauce, chicken broth and cream in a mixing bowl.

2. Use salt and pepper to season the pork shoulder.

3. Set the pot to sauté mode.

4. Add butter and pork into the Instant Pot.

5. Cook for 10 minutes until it gets brown.

6. Add the broth mix, cover and cook on meat for 25 minutes.

7. When time is up do a natural pressure release.

8. Transfer to a plate.

9. Garnish with some lime wedges and parsley.

COOKING TIPS

You can go for readymade teriyaki sauce or make your own at home using pantry staples. Just put soy sauce, garlic, honey, ginger and brown sugar with 1 cup water and simmer over medium heat. Wait for the sauce to thicken to your preference and just add it to the recipe.

Mexican Pork Carnitas

Serving: 4

Cooking time: 45 minutes

Carnitas are one of the most versatile food that goes with almost anything. They are brilliantly crispy and golden on the outside and tender and juicy inside making for a winner recipe! It is as close as it can get to the Mexican flavors and can be prepared at your home in about 45 minutes. You can serve it to the delight of your kids and family who can enjoy a nutritious and sumptuous meal.

NUTRITIONAL VALUES

Calories 355 kcal   Total Carbs 4 g

Fat 29 g   Protein 20 g

INGREDIENTS

1lb. (Boston butt) Pork shoulder

3 cups vegetable / chicken broth

5 tablespoon butter

3 clove garlic, minced

2 teaspoon oregano leaves / cumin

Salt and pepper to taste

For serving:

8 lettuce leaves

Fresh parsley

Lime wedges

DIRECTIONS:

1. Preheat instant pot to meat mode.

2. Meanwhile in a large mixing bowl, add vegetable broth, garlic, oregano/cumin, black pepper and salt.

3. Add 2 tablespoons of butter to the instant pot, add pork and cook for 10 minutes until evenly browned.

4. Now add the prepared broth mixture.

5. Secure the lid and cook on meat mode for about 30 minutes.

6. Once the time is up, do a quick pressure release.

7. Place the cooked pork onto a baking sheet.

8. Shred the pork using two forks.

9. Heat the remaining butter in a non-stick pan over medium to high heat.

10. Add the shredded pork and cook until crispy.

11. Remove and garnish with fresh parsley and lime.

12. It may be served in a lettuce wrap.

COOKING TIPS

You can eat the Mexican pork carnitas in many ways. They can be used as a filling for tortillas, tacos and burritos and ideal for topping in nachos. You can also make a salad and mix it with the carnitas for a healthy and filling meal during lunch or dinner.

Asian Pork Chops

Serving: 4

Cooking time: 20 minutes

Are you bored of making pork chops the same way with the same taste?
Well, today we have something different for you! Today we are going to make Asian pork chops with some teriyaki sauce for unveiling the oriental flavors. The tender and juicy pork chops just melt in your mouth and leave a lingering flavor on your taste buds. It is super simple to make and just needs 20 minutes of your time to prepare.

NUTRITIONAL VALUES

Calories 730 kcal

Fat 59 g

Total Carbs 5 g

Protein 44 g

INGREDIENTS

4 thick pork loin chops, bone-in

½ cup chicken broth

2 cups heavy cream

3 tablespoon butter

1 teaspoon keto teriyaki sauce

Salt and black pepper to taste

DIRECTIONS:

1. Season the chops with black pepper and sauce.

2. Add butter to the pot and choose sauté mode.

3. Add pork chops and cook for 5 minutes.

4. Add chicken broth, cream and teriyaki sauce.

5. Close lid and select manual mode.

6. Cook on high for 15 minutes.

7. Select cancel and carefully do a quick pressure release.

8. Remove the lid and remove the chops.

COOKING TIPS

The Asian pork chops can be served for dinner or lunch with a siding of white rice. It can also be eaten with some mashed potatoes or your favorite salad if you want something green. You can also try out marinating the pork chops with different ingredients such as ginger, garlic and soy sauce.

Ultimate Breakfast Platter

Serving: 4

Cooking time: 30 minutes

Ultimate breakfast platter is a great option to kick start your day with a high dose of energy. It is loaded with 400 calories and 26g protein and comes with the wholeness of eggs and bacon. We have also used fresh tomatoes and mushrooms to enrich the taste and increase the nutritional value. The recipe keeps you satiated for hours to come without feeling the need to snack up from time to time. It also makes for a great brunch!

NUTRITIONAL VALUES

Calories 400 kcal

Fat 29 g

Total Carbs 12 g

Protein 26 g

INGREDIENTS

½ lb of pork sausages

4 bacon slices

1 cup mushrooms

4 ripe tomatoes

8 eggs

1 ½ cups of water

Salt and pepper to taste

DIRECTIONS:

1. Start by frying the cold bacon slices into the Instant pot.

2. Cook bacon on sauté mode until nice and crispy, remove from plate and set aside.

3. In a small mixing bowl, whisk eggs, a tablespoon of water, black pepper and salt, mix until frothy.

4. Add beaten egg to the bacon fat. Add 1 ½ cups of water

5. Cover and cook for about 10 minutes on manual mode.

6. Once the eggs are done, do a quick pressure release.

7. Season tomatoes with salt and pepper.

8. To a small saucepan, add the sausages and keep warm over medium low heat.

9. Add tomatoes and mushrooms to the same pan and cook for 5 minutes.

10. Add a piece of egg, 2 slices of bacon, some mushrooms and tomatoes to the serving plates.

11. Serve with toasted bread.

COOKING TIPS

You can add or omit ingredients from the ultimate breakfast platter according to your preference and wish. The dish can accommodate more veggies if you want and you can try out seasonal ones. You can also replace eggs with egg whites if you are keeping an watch over your diet.

Champions Low-Carb Breakfast

Serving: 4

Cooking time: 20 minutes

We have something for those who are looking to limit their carb intake. The champions low-carb breakfast contains only 5g carbs and makes for a healthy breakfast choice. We have also added avocado the dish which comes with high fiber content and good fats to lower your bad cholesterol. It also contains a bit of potassium and can help you maintain healthy digestive system. This breakfast goes a long way for people on the keto diet.

NUTRITIONAL VALUES

Calories 450 kcal

Fat 41 g

Total Carbs 5 g

Protein 16 g

INGREDIENTS

6 eggs

2 tablespoon butter

2 tablespoon heavy cream

8 bacon slices

1 cup avocado, sliced

1 ½ cups of water

Salt and black pepper to taste

DIRECTIONS:

1. Start by frying the cold bacon slices into the Instant pot on sauté mode.

2. Fry until nice crisp and brown; remove from the pot and set aside.

3. Do not clean the bacon fat from the pot.

4. In a small mixing bowl, whisk eggs, cream, black pepper and salt, mix until frothy.

5. Add butter to the Instant Pot and then beaten eggs. Add 1 ½ cups of water

6. Cover and cook for about 10 minutes on high pressure using manual mode.

7. Once the eggs are done, apply a quick pressure release.

8. Serve the eggs with bacon and sliced avocado.

9. If desired, sprinkle some more salt and pepper.

COOKING TIPS

You are free to experiment with the low-carb breakfast and add more ingredients according to your taste. Some herbs like oregano and rosemary can enhance the flavor and aroma of the dish. You can put them in the mix while adding the butter and the beaten eggs in the instant pot.

Instant Pizza

Who doesn't love pizza? It's a universal food that you can have any time of the day to satisfy your hunger. We have brought an oven-free instant pizza recipe which you can whisk up within 15 minutes. It's much healthier than the takeaway version so you don't need to reach for your phone. Just try out the simple recipe to make mouth watering delicious pizzas for whole of your family. So, round up the ingredients!

NUTRITIONAL VALUES

Calories 440 kcal

Fat 23 g

Total Carbs 41 g

Protein 16 g

INGREDIENTS

10oz. pizza dough or pizza rolls

1/2 cup pizza sauce

3oz pork sausages, sliced

1 medium bell pepper, sliced into rings

3/4 cup mushrooms, sliced

1 cup cheddar cheese, shredded

DIRECTIONS:

1. Grease pizza pan with some oil.

2. Unroll the pizza dough and flatten it with the help of a rolling pin.

3. You may flatten with the palm of your hands; forming a circular shape.

4. Place the prepared dough into the pizza pan.

5. Top the dough with a layer of pizza sauce, sausages, bell pepper, mushrooms and cheese.

6. Cover the pizza with a foil.

7. Pour 1 cup of water into the pan.

8. Place trivet and set the pizza pan over the top of the trivet.

9. Close the lid and set to the manual mode and cook on high for 15 minutes.

10. After time is up, let the pressure release naturally.

11. Carefully slide it out of the pan and cut into slices.

12. Serve hot.

COOKING TIPS

We have used pizza rolls or pizza dough in our recipe. But you can also make your own pizza crust with some bread flour and then bake it on a pizza stone. All-purpose flour will also do the trick- just transfer the crust delicately to the pizza pan. You can also try some different toppings!

Lamb

Portuguese Shanks

Serving: 2

Cooking time: 40 minutes

The meat in lamb shanks can be tough, but the secret to a succulent and flavorful dish lies in slow cooking them. The Portuguese lamb shank is cooked to tenderness with some port wine and tomatoes and just ready to fall off the bones. The recipe uses warm herbs and spices to render an exotic flavor that lingers stays in your mouth. Enjoy a wholesome dish of a lean cut of meat along with some red wine!

NUTRITIONAL VALUES

Calories 780 kcal

Fat 29 g

Total Carbs 26 g

Protein 106 g

INGREDIENTS

2 lamb shanks, weighting 1lb each

1 tbsp. olive oil

2 large onions, diced

5 garlic cloves

2 cups of sweet port wine

1/2 cup chicken stock

1 1/2 tbsp. tomato paste

1/2 can (7oz.) chopped tomatoes

1 tsp. dried thyme

1 tsp. dried rosemary

3 tsp. dried parsley

½ cup beef stock.

sea salt to taste

1 tbsp. unsalted butter

3 tsp. Sherry vinegar

DIRECTIONS:

1. Set to Sauté and add the oil. After browning the lamb shanks, set aside.

2. Set to Sauté and add the onion and garlic to soften them. Set the pot to off mode.

3. Add juices coming from the bowl, wine, chopped tomatoes, stock, tomato paste, herbs, pepper and salt and stir to combine. Add lamb shanks and drop over the liquid to coat them.

4. Place on the cover and set to manual (high) for 30 minutes. Apply natural release. Remove the lamb shanks to a warm dish.

5. Set to Sauté. Add butter and whisk together. Stir in vinegar and pour the sauce over the shanks.

COOKING TIPS

Add a touch of hotness to your sauce with a half tablespoon of chili powder. You can also experiment with other spices to bring a flavor of your choice- the dish is accommodating. The shanks can be served with mashed potatoes and white rice for a full course dinner for your guests.

Lamb Chops in Masala Sauce

Serving: 2
Cooking time: 15 minutes

Fancy something spicy to excite your taste buds? We have brought you a new take on lamb chops that are cooked in masala sauce. It's got the magic of Indian spices which have been traditionally used to roast meat and give it a unique flavor. You can prepare a batch and store them in the fridge as they can be heated easily any time you want. It's great as an appetizer and is breakfast friendly.

NUTRITIONAL VALUES

Calories 625 kcal   Total Carbs 6 g

Fat 27 g   Protein 49 g

INGREDIENTS

1/4 cup Beef Broth

2 lbs (900 g.) Lamb Chops

4 tbsp. Tandoori Masala

1/2 cup Low Fat Plain Yogurt

1 tbsp. Lemon Juice

1 tbsp. (15 g.) Minced Garlic

3 tsb canola oil

1 tsp. (5 g) Cayenne Pepper

Salt and black pepper to taste

DIRECTIONS:

1. Put together and mix yogurt, cream, lemon juice, salt and spices in a bowl.

2. Put lamb chops into the yogurt mix and coat.

3. Marinate chops overnight in the fridge.

4. Add lamb chops and pepper and cook for 5 minutes.

5. Add the rest of the ingredients and cook on high pressure for 15 minutes, followed by a quick release.

COOKING TIPS

We have used Tandoori masala to bring the spicy flavor in this recipe which is easy to get. You can also make your own mix of Indian spices using 1 teaspoon of garam masala, dried fenugreek leaves, ground cumin and ground coriander. Just use it in the place of the Tandoori masala.

British Lamb Ribs

Serving: 2

Cooking time: 15 minutes

Lamb ribs are one of the most delicious ways of eating lamb and doesn't even cost that much. We are going to prepare them in the British style in a rich and creamy sauce. The lamb ribs are cooked to tenderness in the beef broth which also provides it a flavor. It's yummy and cheesy and perfect to serve to your children for dinner or lunch. It's simple to make in a matter of 15 minutes.

NUTRITIONAL VALUES

Calories 540 kcal

Fat 42 g

Total Carbs 3 g

Protein 37 g

INGREDIENTS

1 lb. (450 g.) British Lamb Ribs

1 tbsp. Lime Juice

1/8 cup Olive Oil

1 cup (300 ml) Beef Broth

1 tsp. (5 g.) Paprika

1/4 cup (80 ml) Light Cream

1 tsp. (5 g.) Black Pepper

1/4 cup (100 ml) Shredded Low Fat Cheddar Cheese

Salt, to taste

DIRECTIONS:

1. Mix together salt, black pepper, paprika, lime juice and rub onto the lamb ribs.

2. Heat oil in the Instant Pot and sautéed the ribs until they change colour.

3. Add beef broth and cook on high pressure for 8 minutes. Release pressure naturally.

4. Remove ribs. Add cream and cheese to the Instant Pot. Mix with the leftover broth until cheese is melted.

5. Spoon over ribs and serve.

COOKING TIPS

You can serve the cheesy lamb ribs with kalamata olives and marinated cucumbers to give it a tangy feeling. If you want your sauce more consistent, you can use whipping cream in place of light cream. It mixes with the cheese in the pot and makes for a thicker sauce.

Winter Lamb Stew

Serving: 4

Cooking time: 35 minutes

This lamb stew can be your perfect companion in winter. It is slow cooked in an instant pot till the lamb becomes juicy and tender. The recipe is simple, and you can prepare it in just 35 minutes. The healthy and nutritious dish can be ideal for your dinner or lunch. Just serve it with some bread and you have a wholesome meal on your plates. We have also used some heavy cream and ricotta cheese to raise the consistency of the stew.

NUTRITIONAL VALUES

Calories 730 kcal

Fat 60 g

Total Carbs 5 g

Protein 41 g

INGREDIENTS

1.5lb lamb stew meat

1/4 cup apple
cider vinegar

3/4 cup ricotta cheese

1 cup heavy cream

1/2 cup butter

2 tablespoon all spice powder

For serving:

¼ cup sour cream

Lemon wedges

DIRECTIONS:

1. Set instant pot to sauté mode.

2. Add butter and fry the meat until brown.

3. Add apple cider vinegar, heavy cream and spices.

4. Secure the lid and select manual mode, and set the timer to 30 minutes to cook on high.

5. Once finished cooking, turn the Instant Pot off and let pressure release naturally.

6. Carefully remove the lid and add ricotta cheese, then mix well.

7. Move the stew to a serving bowl and garnish with lemon wedges and serve with sour cream.

COOKING TIPS

You can add an assortment of winter veggies in this stew to make it more nutritious. Some potato or carrots can do the trick without overwhelming the taste and flavor of the original recipe. You can also add a dash of cinnamon and cardamom to enhance the aroma and taste.

Tuscan Lamb Chops

We have given a unique transformation to the traditional lamb chop inspired by Italian cuisine. Just spending half an hour in the kitchen is adequate to cook this tender Tuscan lamb chops. You will only need a few ingredients and some Italian seasoning to bring out the taste. You can have it for your lunch and get a energy boost of 525 calories while cutting back on carbs. It's healthy and perfect for those unexpected guests too!

NUTRITIONAL VALUES

Calories 525 kcal   Total Carbs 8 g

Fat 46 g   Protein 24 g

INGREDIENTS

1.5 lbs lamb chops, bone-in

½ cup tomatoes, chopped

1 ½ cups of water

1 cup coconut cream

2 tablespoon Italian seasoning

3 tablespoon butter

For serving:

Fresh cilantro

DIRECTIONS:

1. Set pot tp sauté mode and heat butter.

2. Place chops and fry until golden.

3. Add coconut cream and Italian seasoning. Add 1 ½ cups of water

4. Lock the lid, setting valve to the sealing position.

5. Cook lamb chops on manual mode (high) for about 20 minutes.

6. Once finished cooking, allow the pot to release pressure naturally.

7. Turn the valve to the venting position and carefully open the lid.

8. Transfer the lamb chops to a serving plate and garnish with cilantro leaves.

COOKING TIPS

You can try out another version of the lamb chops with some cannellini beans. If you want a richer and creamier flavor, then stick to butter beans. Add a dash of chili flakes to the bean mixture to make it a bit spicy and hot! A pinch of rosemary can also stir up the flavor.

Fish & Seafood

Tilapia and Shrimp Paella

Serving: 3
Cooking time: 35 minutes

Paella is a nourishing and filling meal without a hint of pretension. It has held a place of honor in Spanish homes for years, and today we are bringing the recipe just for you! The original paella uses mussels, but we will be making it with tilapia and shrimps. The Spanish flavor is brought about by bell peppers, thyme and onions. The tilapia and shrimp paella is a standalone dish perfect to be served on busy weeknights.

NUTRITIONAL VALUES

Calories 770 kcal

Fat 30 g

Total Carbs 47 g

Protein 75 g

INGREDIENTS

1/2 cup brown rice

1/4 cup quinoa

2 tbsp. lentils

2 tbsp. Sesame seeds

2 1/2 cups of chicken broth

7 oz tilapia fillet

1 cup of shrimps, shelled and deveined

1/2 cup of chopped onions

1 tbsp. garlic, minced

1 tsp. thyme

1 tsp. chili flakes

1 cup of green peas

1 cup of sweet Bell peppers, chopped

2 tbsp. olive oil

Salt and pepper to taste

DIRECTIONS:

1. Wash and chop bell peppers and remove stems and seeds.

2. Pell and chop the onions, peel and mince the garlic.

3. Cut the tilapia fillets into medium-sized pieces.

4. Wash, peel and devein your shrimp.

5. Season tilapia fillets and shrimps with salt and pepper.

6. Set to sauté. Add olive oil and sear fillets and shrimps until fully cooked. Set aside.

7. Rinse brown rice and grains under cold water to wash them away and Drain.

8. Add quinoa, lentils, brown rice, sesame seeds, sweet bell peppers, onions, garlic, thyme, chili flakes, and chicken broth. Stir well.

9. Lock the lid and cook on manual (high) for 25 minutes.

10. Leave for another 10 minutes before releasing pressure.

11. Top with tilapia fillets, shrimp, and green peas prior to serving.

COOKING TIPS

The meal feels really nice along with some nice salad. Use a lot of greens and slice a few onions too. To round it off, grab a bottle of good Spanish red wine imported from the Rioja region. You can also substitute the shrimps in the recipe with littleneck clams.

Tuna Confit Salad

Serving: 3

Cooking time: 4 hours

This is an easy and impressive tuna confit salad recipe. The tuna gets a nice melting texture and tastes heavenly after being slow cooked in the instant pot for 4 hours. The salad is cheesy and filling making it suitable for lunch and dinner. The balsamic vinegar and peppercorns provide a rich flavor to the salad which is further enhanced by the basil leaves. The recipe only needs a few ingredients and comes with a simple cooking process.

NUTRITIONAL VALUES

Calories 500 kcal

Fat 38 g

Total Carbs 5 g

Protein 43 g

INGREDIENTS

1lb raw tuna

2 cups Cherry Tomatoes

1/2 cup Virgin Olive Oil

1 cup Mozzarella Cheese, torn into mini cubes

1 tbsp Pink Peppercorns

1 tbsp Balsamic vinegar

A handful Fresh Basil Leaves

Salt, to taste

DIRECTIONS:

1. Mix raw tuna, tomatoes, peppercorns, and virgin olive oil inside the Instant Pot. Cook on slow cooker mode set on low for 4 hours.

2. Take the tomatoes and the tuna from the pot. Flake the tuna into small pieces and set aside.

3. Take 3 tablespoons of olive oil from the pot. Whisk it with balsamic vinegar in a salad bowl.

4. Drop in the tuna, tomatoes, basil and mozzarella.

5. Season well with salt.

COOKING TIPS

It's a salad, and you can add in your favorite vegetables. Some spinach can be a good choice, but you need to chop it down finely before adding to the pot. You may also put some sweet potatoes and garnish the salad with cilantro leaves to make it even tastier.

Smoked Salmon Avocado Stuffing

Serving: 4

Cooking time: 20 minutes

Get ready to please the crowd with these smoked salmon avocado stuffing! You just need 20 minutes to prepare the dish which can be eaten for lunch or as appetizers. It can also be a quick and easy last minute supper option with the goodness of salmon and avocado. The recipe is perfect for those looking to lose weight as you get lean fat from the salmon. Add to that the health benefits of avocado!

NUTRITIONAL VALUES

Calories 640 kcal

Fat 53 g

Total Carbs 13 g

Protein 31 g

INGREDIENTS

8 eggs

4 avocados

1/2 lb. smoked salmon

1/4 cup butter

1 cup cheddar cheese

1 teaspoon chili flakes

For garnishing:

Fresh parsley, finely chopped

DIRECTIONS:

1. Cut the avocados in half lengthwise and remove the pits.

2. Using a tablespoon scoop out the flesh from each avocado.

3. Mix smoked salmon and avocado together.

4. Scoop the mixture back into the halves. Crack an egg into each avocado cup.

5. Add a teaspoon of butter on the top of each avocado.

6. Sprinkle chili flakes and top with some shredded cheese.

7. Cover with foil.

8. Pour a cup of water into the Instant Pot and place a trivet.

9. Arrange the avocado halves on top of the trivet.

10. Cover with lid and cook on manual mode for about 20 minutes.

11. Once the time is out, do q quick pressure release.

12. Transfer the avocados to a serving bowl.

13. Garnish with some fresh parsley and serve.

COOKING TIPS

You can add a little more chili flakes if you like your stuffed salmon avocados a bit hotter. The butter in the recipe can be replaced with olive oil if you are on a diet. You can also experiment with the garnishing and try out different options such as finely chopped cilantro.

Coconut Fish Curry

Serving: 4

Cooking time: 30 minutes

The recipe is perfect for kids who don't want to eat fish. The rich and creamy curry prepared with salmon or cod is so delicious that your children are sure to gobble it up! You can serve it with some white rice and make way for a filling and healthy dinner. The coconut milk and shredded coconut creates a wonderful flavor which you seldom find in curries. And to top it all, you can make it in just 30 minutes.

NUTRITIONAL VALUES

Calories 700 kcal   Total Carbs 11 g

Fat 57 g   Protein 39 g

INGREDIENTS

1.5-2lbs fish, cod
   or salmon

3 cloves garlic, minced

1 ½ cups of water

1 tablespoon curry powder

2-1/2 cup coconut milk

1/3 cup shredded coconut

4 tablespoon butter

For serving:

Shredded coconut (optional)

DIRECTIONS:

1. Preheat instant pot to sauté mode.

2. Heat butter and add garlic and sauté for about 5 minutes until brown.

3. Add coconut cream and curry powder, cook until mix starts bubbling, (5 minutes).

4. Place the fish into the curry, add shredded coconut and secure the lid. Add 1 ½ cups of water

5. Cook on manual mode for about 10 minutes.

6. Once the fish is done, apply a quick pressure release.

7. Open the lid and spoon out the curry into the serving bowls.

8. If desired sprinkle some more shredded coconut and serve.

COOKING TIPS

You can try different ingredients in the curry to change the taste according to your preference. The curry tastes wonderful with some ginger and lemongrass which increases the richness of the flavor. You can also put in some turmeric to add a nice color to the curry and raise the health benefits.

Salmon with Asparagus

Serving: 4

Cooking time: 10 minutes

We have made it really easy to cook salmon for you in the 10-minute salmon with asparagus recipe. The mayonnaise and Dijon mustard is sure to tingle your taste buds and make the dish delicious as ever. We have also used handsome amount of asparagus which is full of nutrients such as folate, fiber vitamin A, C, E and K. The asparagus is cooked along with the salmon to give you a simple and complete meal.

NUTRITIONAL VALUES

Calories 640 kcal

Fat 52 g

Total Carbs 11 g

Protein 34 g

INGREDIENTS

1/2-1 lb. salmon.

1.5lb asparagus, end trimmed

1 cup cream cheese

6 tablespoon mayonnaise / (1/4 cup of butter can be added)

2 tablespoon Dijon mustard

Juice of 2 lemons

For serving:

Lemon wedges

DIRECTIONS:

1. In a small mixing bowl, mix cream cheese, mayonnaise, mustard and lemon juice.

2. Rub the mixture all over the salmon.

3. Wrap each salmon and 3-4 asparagus stalks into 4 pieces of foil and let marinate for 15 minutes.

4. Pour a cup of water into the instant pot and place the trivet.

5. Place the foil wraps on top of the trivet.

6. Secure the lid and cook on manual mode for 10 minutes (high).

7. Once the fish is done, apply a quick pressure release.

8. Open the lid and transfer the foil-wrapped salmon to a serving plate and serve with lemon wedges.

COOKING TIPS

You can prepare a mix of butter with different herbs according to your choice to make the dish extra rich and flavor-full. Just heat some unsalted butter and mix lemon juice, minced garlic cloves, finely chopped parsley and black pepper. Rub it on the salmon fillets before you place them in the foil.

Citrus Creamy Fish

This recipe will serve your needs when unexpected guests arrive at your house. It can be prepared in only 10 minutes with very few ingredients you find in your home. The rich and creamy fish is so soft that it almost dissolves in your mouth. Your family or guests will love the dish and sure to ask for more! It can serve as an appetizer or you can make a wholesome meal with a side dish of vegetables of your choice.

NUTRITIONAL VALUES

Calories 300 kcal   Total Carbs 3 g

Fat 23 g   Protein 20 g

INGREDIENTS

1lb. white fish fillets

1 teaspoon garlic powder

1 teaspoon onion powder

½ cup cream

1 ½ cups of water

1/4 cup butter

3 tablespoon fresh lemon juice

Salt and black pepper to taste

For garnishing:

Fresh parsley, chopped

Lemon wedges

DIRECTIONS:

1. Melt butter and add garlic powder, onion powder, lemon juice, black pepper and salt.

2. Using paper towel, thoroughly dry excess moisture from fish fillets.

3. Pour the marinade all over the fish, let marinate for 15 minutes.

4. Place the marinated fish and cream into the bottom of the instant pot. Add 1 ½ cups of water

5. Secure lid and set manual mode in high and cook for about 10 minutes.

6. Once cooking time is up, apply quick pressure release.

7. Carefully open the lid and transfer fish to a serving plate.

8. Top with some fresh parsley and lemon wedges.

COOKING TIPS

You can use any variety of whitefish to prepare this dish. The common ones include cod, tilapia, grouper, bass, catfish, haddock, snapper and mullet. You can also wrap each fillet with a Saran wrap and then steam it in the instant pot. Remember to put the skin side down on the wrap for proper smoking.

Parma Lemon Fish

Serving: 4
Cooking time: 10 minutes

Whitefishes are easy to cook and come with several nutritional elements. They are rich in sodium and potassium with your daily requirement of protein. You can also benefit from different types of vitamins such as vitamin A, C and B6 along with moderate levels of calcium, iron and magnesium. All the benefits are available in the Parma lemon fish recipe which can be made in a matter of 10 minutes. It's simple to make with a few ingredients.

NUTRITIONAL VALUES

Calories 520 kcal

Total Carbs 6 g

Fat 43 g

Protein 28 g

INGREDIENTS

1lb. white fish fillets

1 cup Parmesan

1 cup cream

1 ½ cups of water

1/4 cup butter

3 tablespoon fresh lemon juice

1 teaspoon thyme

Salt to taste

For garnishing:

Fresh parsley, chopped

Lemon wedges

DIRECTIONS:

1. Start by preparing marinade; melt butter in a saucepan.

2. Transfer melted butter to a bowl.

3. Add lemon juice, thyme and salt.

4. Place the fish and marinade in a large Ziploc bag. Let marinate for 15 minutes.

5. Transfer the fish and cream into the pot. Add 1 ½ cups of water

6. Secure the lid, setting valve to the sealing position, cook for 10 minutes.

7. When the pot beeps, do a natural pressure release.

8. Open the lid and sprinkle the grated Parmesan.

9. Transfer the fish to the serving plates.

10. Garnish with fresh parsley and lemon wedges.

COOKING TIPS

You can serve the fish with fresh green salad to make a fulfilling lunch or dinner. Other options include having it with some rice or bread- whatever you prefer! You can also add in other herbs like rosemary and grated lemon zest to add more flavors to the dish and enhance the taste.

Beef

Beef Meatballs in Marinara Sauce

The season is just right for a recipe with marinara sauce with the richness of tomato, herbs, garlic and onion. We are going to make beef meatballs and cook them in a tasty marinara sauce. The Italian style meatballs are a classic comfort food which can be prepared well within half an hour. We have enriched the flavor with some pepper, thyme and basil while making the sauce thick with some parmesan or Grana Padano cheese.

NUTRITIONAL VALUES

Calories 500 kcal

Fat 30 g

Total Carbs 18 g

Protein 40 g

INGREDIENTS

- 1 lb. ground beef
- ½ red onion
- 2 garlic minced cloves
- 2 eggs, beaten
- 1 tsp. red chili pepper flakes, or to taste
- 1 tsp salt
- 1 tsp. ground black pepper
- 1 tsp. dried basil
- 1 tsp. dried thyme
- 3 tbsp. Parmesan or Grana Padano cheese, finely grated
- 3 tbsp. olive oil
- 2 ½ cups Marinara sauce (23oz. jar) of choice
- 1/2 cup light chicken stock or water
- 3 tbsp. red wine (optional)
- 1 small bunch fresh parsley, chopped

DIRECTIONS:

1. In a mixing bowl add ingredients except the oil, Marinara sauce, chicken stock and wine. Mix ingredients together with your hands to evenly distribute through the ground beef.

2. Roll the ground beef mix into balls about 2 inches in size. Place them in the refrigerator for 20 minutes.

3. Set to Sauté (high) and add 2 tablespoons of olive oil. When it gets hot sauté the meatballs, in batches, until browned all over. Switch off Sauté.

4. Mix well together Marinara sauce, stock, wine and parsley. Pour ⅓ into the pot, add the meatballs and pour over the remaining sauce.

5. Set to Manual (Normal) for 5 minutes.

6. When time is up, apply a natural release of pressure allow the pressure.

COOKING TIPS

The meatballs can be prepared with any ground meat such as a pound of pork or turkey. It goes along well with a fresh salad and garlic bread. You can also serve it hot over your favorite pasta. You can also make some great meatball sandwiches with the leftover meatballs.

Hungarian Beef Goulash

Serving: 4

Cooking time: 45 minutes

Hungarian beef goulash is arguably the most well-known Hungarian cuisine. It's warm, delicious and hearty enough to be served for dinner on the chilly nights. Chunks of beef are slow cooked to tenderness in beef stock and thick tomato sauce. The paprika, pepper and garlic provide a smoky flavor along with the bell pepper and bay leaves. It's got the right amount of spices to complement the tender, melt in your mouth beef and the tomato sauce.

NUTRITIONAL VALUES

Calories 700 kcal

Fat 42 g

Total Carbs 23 g

Protein 48 g

INGREDIENTS

2 lb. beef steak cut in cubes

4 tbsp. olive oil

2 white onions, sliced

1 green bell pepper, seeded and diced

4 cloves garlic, crushed

4 tbsp. sweet paprika

1 tsp. sea salt

½ tsp black pepper

2 bay leaves

2 tbsp. tomato paste

juice of 1 lemon

1 cup lager beer

1 cup rich beef stock

½ cup sour cream

DIRECTIONS:

1. Season beef cubes with salt and pepper.

2. Set to Sauté and add in the oil. When hot brown, get the beef cubes in batches to avoid overcrowding the pot. Set aside the beef in a bowl.

3. Select Sauté, add the onions and cook until soft. Add the bell pepper and garlic and cook for a further 2 minutes.

4. Add the paprika, salt, pepper, bay leaves, tomato paste, lemon juice, beer and beef stock and stir well to combine. Add browned beef together with any remaining juices from the bowl. Stir to combine.

5. Turn off Sauté and seal the lid.

6. Set the Instant Pot to Manual (high) and cook for 30 minutes.

7. Quick release pressure and remove the lid. Set to Manual (Normal) and cook for a further 10 minutes to thicken sauce.

8. Serve with some sour cream.

COOKING TIPS

Try to arrange some Hungarian sweet paprika as it is the main secret of the taste. You can take your chance with the paprika and add more than 4 spoonfuls to spice it up. Goulash is all about meat and rich broth, so it's better not to add any vegetables.

Sommerset Meatza

Serving: 4

Cooking time: 30 minutes

This dish is high in protein as it comes with the power of beef and eggs with the nutritious aspects of cauliflower. You can give it to your family for lunch or dinner and they are sure to love the delicious recipe. It needs just a few ingredients, so it will take very less time to arrange them. The cooking can be completed in just 30 minutes making it a wholesome and comfort dish for your enjoyment.

NUTRITIONAL VALUES

Calories 700 kcal

Fat 55 g

Total Carbs 8 g

Protein 42 g

INGREDIENTS

1lb. ground beef

1 cup cauliflower

2 large green bell pepper

2 cups cheddar cheese

1 cup mozzarella cheese

2 eggs

Salt and pepper to taste

DIRECTIONS:

1. Remove the top of each pepper and scrape out the ribs and seeds.
2. Cut the pepper into rings and set aside.
3. Cut cauliflower into florets and transfer it to a food processor; pulse until blended.
4. In a large mixing bowl, add ground beef, cauliflower, eggs, black pepper and salt.
5. Using your hands work the mixture together; mix until all the ingredients are evenly combined.
6. Split the meat mixture into 4 even pieces.
7. Use hands to flatten each piece until it is 1/4-inch thick or less. Shape it into a round pizza looking shell.
8. Place the bell pepper rings on top of each pizza and sprinkle cheese.
9. Grease pizza pan with some butter or oil.
10. Transfer pizza to the prepared pan and cover with foil.
11. Pour a cup of water into the pot and set a trivet.
12. Place the pizza pan on top of the trivet.
13. Cover and cook on manual mode for 30 minutes.
14. Once the meatza's are done, do a quick pressure release.
15. Remove from the pot and serve hot.

COOKING TIPS

You need to flatten the meat mixture to a pizza shape shell using your hands. If you find it difficult, you can use a food roller. But you have to be cautious so that you don't end up applying too much pressure- just a gentle press will do the job.

Beef-Stuffed Peppers

Serving: 4

Cooking time: 25 minutes

Your kids will just love the one-dish family friendly meal that you can cook in just 25 minutes. The bell peppers are given a delicious filing made with ground beef over a base of tomato sauce. We have also added a dash of taco seasoning and Worcestershire sauce to bring a mouthwatering flavor and aroma. You can serve the recipe for your meals or have one or two stuffed pepper when you feel hungry.

NUTRITIONAL VALUES

Calories 360 kcal

Fat 13 g

Total Carbs 32 g

Protein 30 g

INGREDIENTS

1 lb ground beef

8 Bell peppers

1 can tomato sauce

1 tablespoon
   Worcestershire sauce

1 tablespoon taco seasoning

For garnishing:

Cilantro, chopped

DIRECTIONS:

1. Remove the top of each pepper and scrape out the ribs and seeds, then set aside.

2. In a large mixing bowl, mix beef, 1/2 can tomato puree, Worcestershire sauce and taco seasoning, mix until well combined.

3. Stuff each pepper with meat mixture.

4. Add the remaining tomato puree to the bottom of the pot and place stuffed pepper over the sauce.

5. Lock the lid into place and cook on manual mode (high) for 25 minutes.

6. Once the pot beeps, do a quick pressure release.

7. Carefully open the lid and transfer the stuffed peppers and sauce to a serving plate.

8. Garnish with chopped cilantro and serve.

COOKING TIPS

The dish can be customized in any way you want to experiment with the taste. You can top the stuffed bell peppers with some shredded cheese before you put them in the instant pot. The cheese melts and creates a rich taste mixing with the stuffed bacon and other ingredients.

Beef & Cheese Stuffed Peppers

Serving: 4
Cooking time: 20 minutes

You can make these beef and cheese stuffed peppers with red, green or yellow bell peppers. It's great to see an assortment of colors topped with mouth watering beef seasoning. The herbs and spices add enriching flavor to the recipe while the cheese form a yummy consistency. The stuffed peppers are low on carbs and high on protein and energy and made with a simple cooking process. And best of all, you can make it ready within 20 minutes.

NUTRITIONAL VALUES

Calories 725 kcal

Fat 62 g

Total Carbs 12 g

Protein 30 g

INGREDIENTS

1 lb ground beef

8 Bell peppers

1 1/2 cups cheddar cheese

1 teaspoon paprika

1 teaspoon oregano

3 tablespoon olive oil

Salt and black pepper to taste

DIRECTIONS:

1. Get rid of the top of each pepper and scrape out the ribs and seeds, set aside.

2. In a large mixing bowl, mix beef, paprika, oregano, black pepper and salt; mix until combined.

3. Stuff each pepper with beef mixture and drizzle oil.

4. Top each pepper with cheddar cheese.

5. Wrap each pepper with aluminum foil

6. Add a cup of water into the bottom of the pot.

7. Place a trivet and place the previously prepared peppers over it.

8. Lock the lid, turning valve position to the sealing, cook on high for 20 minutes on manual mode.

9. Once finished cooking, use a quick pressure release.

10. Carefully open the lid and transfer the stuffed peppers onto a serving plate.

COOKING TIPS

You can try out quite a few variations of this dish. You can add mozzarella cheese and pizza blend of shredded cheddar for the topping. You can also make a sauce from crushed tomatoes or tomato puree to go along with the stuffed beef peppers. Add a bit of chili flakes if you want!

Tijuana Chili Beef

Serving: 4

Cooking time: 35 minutes

You can make a complete meal in your instant pot with this Tijuana chili beef and return home for a hot and tasty meal. The Mexican style dish combines ground beef, onions and tomato puree all nestled together in your slow cooker to bring a delicious taste. We have also added some kidney beans which are rich in protein, fiber and carbs. It also makes the dish more filling so that you don't have to cook anything else.

NUTRITIONAL VALUES

Calories 450 kcal

Fat 11 g

Total Carbs 55 g

Protein 40 g

INGREDIENTS

1lb ground beef

1 medium onion, chopped

1 can tomato puree

2 can red kidney beans

1 tablespoon red chili powder

1 tablespoon cumin

1 tablespoon oil

Salt to taste

For topping:

1 pack tortilla chips

½ cup sour cream

½ cup cheddar cheese, shredded

DIRECTIONS:

1. Select sauté mode on your pot.

2. Heat oil until shimmering, add onion and sauté for 5 minutes.

3. Add beef and brown for 10 minutes.

4. Add in the remaining ingredients with a 1/2 cup of water.

5. Cover the lid and set pot to the manual mode; cook for 30 minutes in high.

6. Once the cooking time is up, apply a quick pressure release.

7. Transfer the chili to a serving dish.

8. Sprinkle some cheese and top with sour cream.

9. Serve with tortillas.

COOKING TIPS

You can try out a few toppings as per your liking. Some red peppers and sliced green jalapenos will be perfect to go along with the chili. You can also add a plate of mashed potatoes by the side and make it suitable for lunch or dinner for your family.

Creamy Chili with Beef

Serving: 4

Cooking time: 35 minutes

This chili recipe is easy to make and can be yours within 35 minutes. We haven't used any fancy ingredient and kept them to a minimum without compromising on the taste. The rich and creamy beef chili is perfect for the fall and winter nights as well as the big game days! It goes well along with some tortillas or bread and makes for a hot and delicious dinner or lunch. So, let's get going!

NUTRITIONAL VALUES

Calories 430 kcal

Fat 37 g

Total Carbs 6 g

Protein 17 g

INGREDIENTS

1lb ground beef

1 medium onion, chopped

1 cup cherry tomatoes, halved

3 cloves garlic, minced

1 tablespoon butter

1 tablespoon red chili powder

1 tablespoon cumin

Salt to taste

For topping:

½ cup sour cream

½ cup cheddar cheese, shredded

DIRECTIONS:

1. Preheat Instant pot to sauté mode.

2. Heat butter and add onion, sauté for 5 minutes.

3. Add garlic, cook stirring constantly for 1 minute.

4. Now add in the beef and brown for 10 minutes.

5. Once the beef is browned, add tomatoes, red chili powder, cumin, 1/2 cup of water and salt.

6. Close the lid and cook on manual mode for 20 minutes in high.

7. Once the meat is done, release the pressure naturally.

8. Transfer the beef mixture to a serving bowl.

9. Top with some cheese and serve with a dollop of sour cream.

COOKING TIPS

We have used simple ingredients in the recipe to make your job easy. But you can go ahead and try out some variations like adding corn or beans to the chili to give it some extra body. You can also add more chili powder if you want your dish to be hotter.

Instant Beef Steaks

Serving: 4

Cooking time: 35 minutes

How about some beef steak you can cook in around 30 minutes? It requires no oven and you can easily get delicious results without breaking a sweat. We have used instant pot to create tender and juicy steak with rich flavor brought about by rosemary, oregano and Worcestershire sauce. You can prepare this quickly for dinner and your whole family will be pleasantly surprised! We have only used six to seven ingredients which can be found right in your kitchen.

NUTRITIONAL VALUES

Calories 310 kcal

Fat 24 g

Total Carbs 3 g

Protein 20 g

INGREDIENTS

1lb Beef rib-eye steaks, 1-1/2 inch thick

3 clove garlic, minced

2 tablespoon Worcestershire sauce

1 teaspoon hot sauce

1 tablespoon rosemary

1 teaspoon oregano

3 tablespoon white wine vinegar

For serving:

Roasted potatoes, cubed

DIRECTIONS:

1. Start by preparing a marinade for steaks.

2. In a small mixing bowl, mix garlic, Worcestershire sauce, hot sauce, rosemary, oregano and vinegar.

3. Pour the marinade over the steaks and marinate for 30 minutes.

4. Turn the Instant pot on.

5. Carefully place the marinated steaks into the pot.

6. Cover and set the valve to the sealing position.

7. Cook on manual mode for about 35 minutes (high).

8. Once time is up, apply quick release.

9. Transfer the steaks to a serving dish.

10. Serve with roasted potatoes.

COOKING TIPS

The instant beef steak is a wholesome meal for your family. But if you want you can add some vegetables on the go. Just boil some chopped carrots and beans and add them on the plate while you serve the steak. If you want, you can also eat it with a cup of rice.

Garlic Beef Steaks

Serving: 4

Cooking time: 35 minutes

We have something for a mouth-watering change of taste for your next party! Take your normal steak to a new flavor height by cooking the beef with a garlic-y blend which can be made in 35 minutes. We have also enriched the flavor of the steak by adding some rosemary, oregano and Worcestershire sauce. The recipe is perfect for those on a low carb or keto diet as it contains only 3g of carbohydrates.

NUTRITIONAL VALUES

Calories 410 kcal

Fat 35 g

Total Carbs 3 g

Protein 20 g

INGREDIENTS

1lb. Beef rib-eye steaks, 1-1/2 inch thick

4 tablespoon butter

2 tablespoon Worcestershire sauce

1 tablespoon rosemary

1 teaspoon oregano

3 tablespoon lemon juice

For serving:

Roasted asparagus

Sautéed mushrooms

DIRECTIONS:

1. Start by preparing a marinade for steaks, in a small mixing bowl, mix butter, Worcestershire sauce, rosemary, oregano and lemon juice.

2. Rub the marinade all over the steaks and let marinate for 1/2 an hour.

3. Place the marinated steaks into the Instant pot.

4. Cover and cook on manual mode for 35 minutes in high

5. When the timer is up, allow the pressure to release naturally.

6. Transfer the steaks to a serving plate.

7. If desired serve with sautéed mushrooms and asparagus.

COOKING TIPS

Steaks can be eaten as they are or you can some side dish to go along with it. The traditional sidings of mashed potatoes and veggies are a great addition to your lunch or dinner. You can also add a tablespoon of butter to the marinate and mix it with the beef.

Vegetarian

Lebanese Zucchini Shakshuka

Serving: 2
Cooking time: 10 minutes

Shakshuka is popular as an egg-based dinner recipe, but it's eaten in Israel as breakfast to give a spicy start to the day. Shakshuka can be made in your instant pot at once by baking eggs over a sauce of tomatoes spiced with pepper, paprika and cumin. In this recipe, we have used the nutritious zucchinis to add base and make the dish a complete one so that you can have it for breakfast or even for a quick lunch.

NUTRITIONAL VALUES

Calories 660 kcal

Fat 55 g

Total Carbs 25 g

Protein 23 g

INGREDIENTS

1 large Zucchini, spiralized or cut into thin strips

1 White Onion, diced

1 large Red Bell Pepper, diced

3 cloves Garlic, finely minced

1 tsp. Paprika

1 tsp. Cumin Powder

14 oz can Diced Tomatoes

¼ cup Vegetable Stock

4 Eggs

1 tbsp. Olive Oil

Salt, to taste

Pepper, to taste

DIRECTIONS:

1. Set to sauté mode.

2. Heat up olive oil.

3. Sauté the onions, garlic, and bell pepper. Do this until onions are very clear.

4. Add zucchini and sauté for 2 minutes.

5. Drop diced tomatoes, paprika, cumin, and vegetable stock. Simmer for 4 minutes.

6. Season with salt and pepper.

7. Make a dent over the vegetables for each egg.

8. Crack each whole egg into each dent.

9. Switch Instant Pot to keep warm setting and leave for 5 minutes.

COOKING TIPS

Shakshuka can be made with any vegetable of your choice. You can try a version with eggplants which tastes wonderful. Serve the dish with challah bread to suck up the juices. The dish also goes along well with a quickly put together salad comprising of greens and other colorful veggies.

Cauliflower and Broccoli Bake

Serving: 4
Cooking time: 15 minutes

You must have seen many recipes of broccoli and cauliflower casserole. Today we are going to make this nutritious and healthy dish in an instant pot. You just need a few ingredients and the simple cooking process gets over in just 15 minutes. It tastes lovely with the creamy mozzarella cheese and addition of heavy cream that just melts in your mouth. The high energy recipe is perfect for breakfast while you can also carry it to work for lunch.

NUTRITIONAL VALUES

Calories 720 kcal   Total Carbs 12 g

Fat 59 g   Protein 39 g

INGREDIENTS

1lb. cauliflower, shredded

1/2 lb. broccoli, shredded

1 cups of water

4 cup mozzarella cheese

2 cups heavy cream

6 tablespoon butter

DIRECTIONS:

1. Preheat the pot on sauté mode.

2. Add shredded cauliflower and broccoli into the pot. Add 1 cup of water

3. Add butter, seal the lid and cook in high pressure for 10 minutes.

4. Once the cooking is done add in cheese and heavy cream, cook for another 5 minutes.

5. Once cooked, transfer to a serving dish and present immediately.

COOKING TIPS

You can use a variety of cheese in the broccoli and cauliflower bake recipe. Some parmesan cheese will be great to increase the consistency of the dish making it more filling. You can also add some Italian seasoning or herbs of your choice to get your desired taste and flavor.

Creamy Pasta

We are going to cook this rich and creamy pasta with zucchinis noodles made with a spiralizer. Zucchinis are nutritious and healthy and contain magnesium, potassium, fiber, phosphorus, calcium, riboflavin and vitamin C. They also come with iron, zinc, sodium and vitamins A, E, K and B6. Zucchinis also help you feel satiated making this dish a great choice for breakfast or lunch. We will need few simple ingredients and you can cook it in just 15 minutes.

NUTRITIONAL VALUES

Calories 340 kcal   Total Carbs 4 g

Fat 29 g   Protein 17 g

INGREDIENTS

3 large zucchinis,

½ cup butter

1 cup mozzarella cheese, shredded

1 cup parmesan cheese, shredded

½ cup milk

Salt and black pepper to taste

For serving:

Parmesan cheese, grated

DIRECTIONS:

1. Wash the zucchini and trim the ends off. Using a spiralizer, create zucchini "noodles".

2. Select sauté mode on the instant pot.

3. Melt butter and add milk, salt and black pepper. Bring milk to a boil.

4. Once milk starts to bubble, add cheddar, mozzarella and parmesan cheese, then whisk until well combined.

5. Add zucchini noodles and cook for 5 minutes.

6. Just coat the noodles with cheese but avoid cooking for too long to avoid getting them soggy.

7. Once the noodles are warm and well mixed, present the dish in a large serving plate.

8. Sprinkle some more parmesan on top if desired.

COOKING TIPS

You can use aluminum foils to retain the moistness of the pasta. Foils also ensure that the food is cooked evenly while making clean up easier. You can also store the leftover in foils and eat it later. The dish can also be cooked with different seasoning meant for vegetables.

Vegetarian Lasagna

Serving: 4

Cooking time: 20 minutes

We wanted to create the best vegetable lasagna recipe and have come up with this! The lasagna is loaded with vegetables and retains rich cheesiness in all of the layers. This can be a good way to make your kids eat their vegetables as it just tastes delicious. Your family will not miss the meat with this vegetable lasagna that is prepared with healthy zucchinis and eggplant. The recipe can be prepared in just 20 minutes.

NUTRITIONAL VALUES

Calories 725 kcal

Fat 61 g

Total Carbs 18 g

Protein 30 g

INGREDIENTS

1 large eggplant, sliced

1 large zucchini, sliced

1 1/2 cups of water

1 cup marinara sauce

2 cheddar cheese, shredded

2 cups heavy cream

DIRECTIONS:

1. Place the eggplant and zucchini slices in a spring foam pan

2. Add cream, marinara sauce and cheese.

3. Repeat until making 3 layers using all the ingredients.

4. Place the spring foam pan into the bottom of the pot and cook on manual mode for 20 minutes, choosing high. Add 1 ½ cups of water.

5. After finishing, apply a quick pressure release.

6. Serve hot.

COOKING TIPS

You may add in your choice of vegetables in the lasagna. Some bell peppers and carrots can do the trick but you have to chop them to small pieces. Just add them with the eggplant and zucchinis in the spring foam pan before you put in the cream and marinara sauce.

Champions Breakfast Hash

Serving: 4
Cooking time: minutes

This easy to make vegetarian breakfast will kick start your day with a high dose of energy. It is perfect for those watching their carb intake coming with only 8g of carbohydrate. We have used turnips which lowers your blood pressure, reduces inflammation, fights cancer and keeps you feeling full for a long time. The recipe also contains shallots which improve your blood circulation, maintains good cholesterol levels, reduces risk if cancer and decreases blood pressure.

NUTRITIONAL VALUES

Calories 550 kcal

Fat 45 g

Total Carbs 8 g

Protein 29 g

INGREDIENTS

10 Whole Eggs, beaten

6 oz diced Turnips

4 tbsp Diced Shallots

1/2 cup Cheddar Cheese

2 tbsp Avocado Oil (also 8 teaspoons for serving)

DIRECTIONS:

1. Set Pot to sauté function.

2. Heat a tablespoon of avocado oil.

3. Drop shallots and turnips. Sauté until caramelized.

4. Stir in the beaten eggs and leave until completely cooked.

5. Add salt and pepper to taste.

6. Turn off the heat and sprinkle in the cheese.

7. Drizzle avocado oil.

COOKING TIPS

You can experiment with the vegetables and add your own assortment easily in this breakfast recipe. It will also go along well with some toasted bread to make a wholesome meal or brunch. If you want to have it with less fat content, you can only add the white part of the eggs.

Spinach Mushroom Frittata

This spinach mushroom frittata is quick and easy to make and ideal for a fancy brunch or a busy weekday dinner. Using a few simple ingredients like spinach and mushroom you can make this delicious recipe in your own way. It's high on energy and protein while being low on carbs and fat. You can put it in the instant pot and go upstairs to get your kids ready for school while the dish is prepared.

NUTRITIONAL VALUES

Calories 350 kcal

Fat 25 g

Total Carbs 10 g

Protein 23 g

INGREDIENTS

1-1/2 cup mushrooms, sliced

1lb. fresh spinach, chopped

1-1/2 cup red bell pepper, chopped

1 cup cheddar cheese, shredded

1/3 cup heavy cream

8 eggs

Salt and pepper to taste

DIRECTIONS:

1. Grease a 7-inch pan with some oil.

2. Use a mixing bowl to stir all the ingredients together.

3. Pour the mix into the prepared pan, cover with foil.

4. Add a cup of water to the Instant Pot and place a trivet.

5. Now place the prepared pan on top of the trivet, secure the lid, setting valve to sealing position.

6. Select manual and cook for 20 minutes.

7. Once the frittata is done, apply a quick pressure release.

8. Carefully remove the pan from the pot and invert the frittata onto a serving plate and serve.

COOKING TIPS

We have used spinach and mushroom for this frittata, but you are free to try out your favorite vegetables. The frittata maintains its flavor and texture so that you can reheat and have it anytime you please. You can also add in some chopped onions to enhance the flavor and taste.

Broccoli Muffins

Serving: 4
Cooking time: 15 minutes

Do your kids always throw a tantrum every time you give them broccoli to eat? Well, this broccoli muffin recipe can be the best thing to get them to eat the nutritious vegetable. Your family can also get a break from having the regular muffins and taste a completely new recipe. It is surely going to be a hit with your family and guests and become a favorite addition to your menu of vegetarian items.

NUTRITIONAL VALUES

Calories 450 kcal   Total Carbs 7 g

Fat 38 g   Protein 21 g

INGREDIENTS

8 eggs   **For topping:**

1 1/2 cup cheddar cheese   Whipped cream

1 cup heavy cream

1 head broccoli, finely chopped

2 cloves garlic, minced

1 teaspoon oregano

Salt and black pepper

DIRECTIONS:

1. Grease 4 ovenproof cups with butter.

2. In a large mixing bowl, whisk eggs, cream, garlic, oregano, black pepper and salt.

3. Stir in broccoli and cheddar cheese.

4. Pour 1 cup of water into the instant pot and place a trivet.

5. Pour the egg mixture into the prepared cups.

6. Place the cups on top of the trivet.

7. Select high pressure and cook for 15 minutes.

8. Once the muffins are done, let pressure release naturally.

9. Carefully open the lid and remove the cups.

10. Serve with a dollop of cream.

COOKING TIPS

You can store the broccoli muffins in your freezer or fridge for even a week without any issues. Just heat them up a bit when you are feeling hungry and have them on the go! The muffins can also be customized with different toppings and add-ons as per your preference.

Giant Pancake

Serving: 4

Cooking time: 20 minutes

Pancakes are an all-time favorite which can be enjoyed any time of the day. We have a brand-new recipe for making a giant pancake using instant pot. We are using just five ingredients which can be easily found in your kitchen for a quick and simple cooking. You can make the pancakes ready in just 20 minutes and serve them hot to your kids and hubby. They are great for your breakfast and can be suitable for the snacks time.

NUTRITIONAL VALUES

Calories 375 kcal

Fat 12 g

Total Carbs 56 g

Protein 10 g

INGREDIENTS

2 cup all-purpose flour

1 1/3 cup coconut milk

2 eggs

1 teaspoon baking powder or
½ teaspoon baking soda

3 tablespoon sugar

For topping:

1 cup mixed berries

Banana, sliced

Maple syrup

DIRECTIONS:

1. In a large mixing bowl, whisk eggs and milk, mix until well combined.

2. Add in the remaining ingredients and whisk again.

3. Now grease the inside of the instant pot with butter.

4. Pour the pancake mixture and secure with cover. Add ½ cups of water

5. Select manual mode and cook for 20 minutes on high.

6. When time is up, quick release pressure.

7. Once the pancake is done, loosen the edges and transfer it to a serving plate.

8. Top with some sliced banana and mixed berries.

9. Drizzle maple syrup and serve.

COOKING TIPS

You can make pancakes anyway you want but we have provided a simple recipe. You can add in more stuff and experiment with the toppings. You may add different fruits like apples and even add a bit of Nutella for a chocolaty flavor- just as your kids will love it!

Cottage Berry Pancake

Serving: 4
Cooking time: 20 minutes

We have yet another variation of all-time favorite pancakes. This time we will be making the pancakes with cottage cheese with the yumminess of strawberries. Your kids and family will just fall for this and you can quickly make the pancakes in 20 minutes. We have used coconut oil in our recipe which gives a sweet flavor to the pancakes with a coconut-y aroma. There're only a few ingredients to arrange so let's get started!

NUTRITIONAL VALUES

Calories 320 kcal   Total Carbs 7 g

Fat 26 g   Protein 17 g

INGREDIENTS

1 1/2 cup cottage cheese

5 eggs

1/2 cups of water

1 1/2 tablespoon coconut flour

5 tablespoon coconut oil

1 package stevia

1 cup strawberries, sliced

DIRECTIONS:

1. In a large mixing bowl, whisk eggs, cottage cheese, coconut flour, and stevia, mix until well combined.

2. Press sauté mode on the instant pot.

3. Add coconut oil to the pot.

4. Pour the pancake mixture and secure the lid with vent closed. Add ½ cups of water.

5. Select manual mode and cook for about 20 minutes in high.

6. Once the pancake is done do quick pressure release.

7. Loosen the sides with the help of spatula.

8. Top the pancake strawberries and serve.

COOKING TIPS

We have used stevia to add sweetness to the pancake in place of sugar. But you are free to use any sweetener or sugar if you want. You can also try out a few toppings along with strawberries. The best topping will be combining your favorite berries and have it with the pancakes.

Carrot & Potato Soup

Serving: 4

Cooking time: 30 minutes

The fall and winter are perfect time for soups and comfort food. We are presenting a carrot and potato soup to go well along with the crispy weather and provide the nutrition you need. The soup is creamy, filling and delicious while being light at the same time. It is great for a weeknight dinner and can save you from the untimely hunger pangs during the day. The soup is easy to make with some simple ingredients.

NUTRITIONAL VALUES

Calories 370 kcal   Total Carbs 57 g

Fat 12 g   Protein 12 g

INGREDIENTS

1 head broccoli, chopped

2 large carrots, sliced

3 potatoes, cubed

5 cups vegetable broth

1/2 cup heavy cream

Salt and pepper to taste

For garnishing:

Fresh parsley leaves

DIRECTIONS:

1. Place all the ingredients into the Instant Pot, except cream.

2. Secure the lid into the place and cook on high for 30 minutes.

3. Once time is up, apply a quick pressure release.

4. Remove the lid and stir in the cream.

5. Mix well, and ladle the soup into the bowls, drizzle a spoonful of cream on top of each serving.

6. Garnish with some fresh parsley and serve.

COOKING TIPS

You can try out different flavors with spices and herbs in the carrot and potato soup. Some white pepper will bring a nice flavor and a bit of paprika can lead to a richer color. You can avoid using the cream if you are looking to reduce your fat intake.

Broccoli Soup

This broccoli soup is a favorite easy and quick meal you can have throughout the year. It's healthy and gives you a delicious way to eat your vegetables. You can prepare it within 20 minutes using a few simple ingredients. The soup is rich and creamy as we have used heavy cream and cheddar cheese and comes with a comforting consistency. You can have it as a quick dinner or lunch without having to cook all day long!

NUTRITIONAL VALUES

Calories 460 kcal   Total Carbs 6 g

Fat 42 g   Protein 18 g

INGREDIENTS

5 cups broccoli

4 cup vegetable broth

1 cup heavy cream

2 cup cheddar cheese

4 clove garlic, minced

Salt to taste

DIRECTIONS:

1. Clean and cut the broccoli into florets.

2. Roughly chop florets into small pieces.

3. You may process in a food processor until small-rice sized pieces.

4. Except cheese, mix all the ingredients into the instant pot.

5. Secure the lid and set valve to the sealing.

6. Select manual mode and cook on high for 20 minutes.

7. Once the pot beeps, apply a quick pressure release.

8. Carefully open the lid and stir in cheese.

9. Transfer the broccoli to the serving bowls and serve.

COOKING TIPS

You can experiment with different type of seasoning for this soup. Some Italian seasoning will bring out new flavors while you can also add a bit of thyme to the mix. Serve it with a bread of loaf or toasts for a complete comfort meal for your family and kids.

Weekly Schedules

I hope you have enjoyed the recipes in this book so far. Including a variety of ingredients , I hope the meals will add flavour to your breakfasts, lunches and dinners, for a long time. As these recipes are ideal for beginners, together with the instructions on how to use the Instant Pot included in the first pages, you have plenty of material to enjoy whether you are complete beginner or an advanced user.

Having this in mind, because the large variety of recipes, I have compiled 1000 days of Instant Pot Recipes. Every weekly schedule includes three meals for each day, so you know in advance what to cook and planning, while maintaining variety in your meals. SO not you know, get ready for a stress-free Instant Pot meal planning!

WEEK 1	MONDAY	TUESDAY	WEDNESDAY	THURSDAY	FRIDAY	SATURDAY	SUNDAY
MEAL 1	Lemongrass braised chicken	Creamy Chicken Pie	Beef-Stuffed Peppers	American Barbecue Turkey	Hungarian beef goulash	Sommerset Meatza	Beef & Cheese Stuffed Peppers
MEAL 2	Turkey Meatballs	Japanese Balsamic Pork Roast	Broccoli Soup	Spinach Mushroom Frittata	Creamy Chili with Beef	Instant Carrot Chicken Pie	Cauliflower Chicken Rice
MEAL 3	Japanese Balsamic Pork Roast	Tuna Confit Salad	Hungarian beef goulash	Hungarian beef goulash	Tilapia and shrimp paella	American Barbecue Turkey	American Barbecue Turkey

WEEK 2	MONDAY	TUESDAY	WEDNESDAY	THURSDAY	FRIDAY	SATURDAY	SUNDAY
MEAL 1	Spicy roasted chicken	Lebanese Zucchini Shakshuka	Portobello Turkey legs	Beef meatballs in Marinara Sauce	Tilapia and shrimp paella	Pork Roast in Honey and garlic	Portuguese Shanks
MEAL 2	Portobello Turkey legs	Beef meatballs in Marinara Sauce	Spicy roasted chicken	Lebanese Zucchini Shakshuka	Pork Roast in Honey and garlic	Tilapia and shrimp paella	Portuguese Shanks
MEAL 3	Pork Roast in Honey and garlic	Lebanese Zucchini Shakshuka	Beef meatballs in Marinara Sauce	Tilapia and shrimp paella	Portuguese Shanks	Portobello Turkey legs	Spicy roasted chicken

WEEK 3	MONDAY	TUESDAY	WEDNESDAY	THURSDAY	FRIDAY	SATURDAY	SUNDAY
MEAL 1	Portuguese Shanks	Tilapia and shrimp paella	Lebanese Zucchini Shakshuka	Beef meatballs in Marinara Sauce	Spicy roasted chicken	Pork Roast in Honey and garlic	Portobello Turkey legs
MEAL 2	Tilapia and shrimp paella	Lebanese Zucchini Shakshuka	Beef meatballs in Marinara Sauce	Portuguese Shanks	Pork Roast in Honey and garlic	Portobello Turkey legs	Spicy roasted chicken
MEAL 3	Beef meatballs in Marinara Sauce	Spicy roasted chicken	Portobello Turkey legs	Pork Roast in Honey and garlic	Portuguese Shanks	Tilapia and shrimp paella	Lebanese Zucchini Shakshuka

WEEK 4	MONDAY	TUESDAY	WEDNESDAY	THURSDAY	FRIDAY	SATURDAY	SUNDAY
MEAL 1	Lebanese Zucchini Shakshuka	Beef meatballs in Marinara Sauce	Tilapia and shrimp paella	Portuguese Shanks	Pork Roast in Honey and garlic	Portobello Turkey legs	Spicy roasted chicken
MEAL 2	Hainanese Chicken	Balsamic Turkey Meatballs	Cauliflower and Broccoli Bake	Popeye Frittata	Hungarian beef goulash	Lamb Chops in Masala Sauce	Tuna Confit Salad
MEAL 3	Balsamic Turkey Meatballs	Hainanese Chicken	Popeye Frittata	Lamb Chops in Masala Sauce	Tuna Confit Salad	Hungarian beef goulash	Cauliflower and Broccoli Bake

WEEK 5	MONDAY	TUESDAY	WEDNESDAY	THURSDAY	FRIDAY	SATURDAY	SUNDAY
MEAL 1	Popeye Frittata	Balsamic Turkey Meatballs	Hainanese Chicken	Cauliflower and Broccoli Bake	Hungarian beef goulash	Tuna Confit Salad	Lamb Chops in Masala Sauce
MEAL 2	Lamb Chops in Masala Sauce	Cauliflower and Broccoli Bake	Hungarian beef goulash	Tuna Confit Salad	Popeye Frittata	Balsamic Turkey Meatballs	Hainanese Chicken
MEAL 3	Tuna Confit Salad	Hungarian beef goulash	Cauliflower and Broccoli Bake	Lamb Chops in Masala Sauce	Hainanese Chicken	Popeye Frittata	Balsamic Turkey Meatballs

WEEK 6	MONDAY	TUESDAY	WEDNESDAY	THURSDAY	FRIDAY	SATURDAY	SUNDAY
MEAL 1	Hungarian beef goulash	Tuna Confit Salad	Balsamic Turkey Meatballs	Popeye Frittata	Lamb Chops in Masala Sauce	Cauliflower and Broccoli Bake	Hainanese Chicken
MEAL 2	Cauliflower and Broccoli Bake	Popeye Frittata	Lamb Chops in Masala Sauce	Balsamic Turkey Meatballs	Tuna Confit Salad	Hainanese Chicken	Hungarian beef goulash
MEAL 3	Lemongrass braised chicken	Bacon-Stuffed Avocados	American Barbecue Turkey	British Lamb Ribs	Smoked Salmon Avocado Stuffing	Creamy Pasta	Sommerset Meatza

WEEK 7	MONDAY	TUESDAY	WEDNESDAY	THURSDAY	FRIDAY	SATURDAY	SUNDAY
MEAL 1	American Barbecue Turkey	British Lamb Ribs	Smoked Salmon Avocado Stuffing	Bacon-Stuffed Avocados	Creamy Pasta	Lemongrass braised chicken	Creamy Pasta
MEAL 2	Bacon-Stuffed Avocados	Smoked Salmon Avocado Stuffing	American Barbecue Turkey	Lemongrass braised chicken	Sommerset Meatza	Smoked Salmon Avocado Stuffing	Bacon-Stuffed Avocados
MEAL 3	British Lamb Ribs	Japanese Balsamic Pork Roast	Smoked Salmon Avocado Stuffing	Creamy Pasta	Bacon-Stuffed Avocados	Sommerset Meatza	American Barbecue Turkey

WEEK 8	MONDAY	TUESDAY	WEDNESDAY	THURSDAY	FRIDAY	SATURDAY	SUNDAY
MEAL 1	Smoked Salmon Avocado Stuffing	Creamy Pasta	Lamb Chops in Masala Sauce	Sommerset Meatza	British Lamb Ribs	American Barbecue Turkey	Bacon-Stuffed Avocados
MEAL 2	Sommerset Meatza	American Barbecue Turkey	Bacon-Stuffed Avocados	Lemongrass braised chicken	Creamy Pasta	Smoked Salmon Avocado Stuffing	British Lamb Ribs
MEAL 3	Creamy Pasta	Lemongrass braised chicken	Japanese Balsamic Pork Roast	British Lamb Ribs	Bacon-Stuffed Avocados	American Barbecue Turkey	Smoked Salmon Avocado Stuffing

WEEK 9	MONDAY	TUESDAY	WEDNESDAY	THURSDAY	FRIDAY	SATURDAY	SUNDAY
MEAL 1	Creamy Italian Chicken	Winter Lamb Stew	Turkey Meatballs	Coconut Fish Curry	Mexican Pork Carnitas	Beef & Cheese Stuffed Peppers	Vegetarian Lasagna
MEAL 2	Turkey Meatballs	Japanese Balsamic Pork Roast	Creamy Italian Chicken	Winter Lamb Stew	Vegetarian Lasagna	Coconut Fish Curry	Beef-Stuffed Peppers
MEAL 3	Japanese Balsamic Pork Roast	Turkey Meatballs	Coconut Fish Curry	Creamy Italian Chicken	Beef-Stuffed Peppers	Winter Lamb Stew	Vegetarian Lasagna

WEEK 10	MONDAY	TUESDAY	WEDNESDAY	THURSDAY	FRIDAY	SATURDAY	SUNDAY
MEAL 1	Winter Lamb Stew	Creamy Italian Chicken	Japanese Balsamic Pork Roast	Vegetarian Lasagna	Coconut Fish Curry	Turkey Meatballs	Beef-Stuffed Peppers
MEAL 2	Coconut Fish Curry	Winter Lamb Stew	Vegetarian Lasagna	Turkey Meatballs	Beef-Stuffed Peppers	Creamy Italian Chicken	Japanese Balsamic Pork Roast
MEAL 3	Beef-Stuffed Peppers	Creamy Italian Chicken	Coconut Fish Curry	Vegetarian Lasagna	Winter Lamb Stew	Japanese Balsamic Pork Roast	Turkey Meatballs

WEEK 11	MONDAY	TUESDAY	WEDNESDAY	THURSDAY	FRIDAY	SATURDAY	SUNDAY
MEAL 1	Vegetarian Lasagna	Coconut Fish Curry	Japanese Balsamic Pork Roast	Beef-Stuffed Peppers	Turkey Meatballs	Winter Lamb Stew	Creamy Italian Chicken
MEAL 2	Rotisserie Chicken	Sausage & Veggie Muffins	Mexican Pork Carnitas	Tuscan Lamb Chops	Salmon with Asparagus	Beef & Cheese Stuffed Peppers	Champions Breakfast Hash
MEAL 3	Sausage & Veggie Muffins	Rotisserie Chicken	Tuscan Lamb Chops	Mexican Pork Carnitas	Champions Breakfast Hash	Salmon with Asparagus	Beef & Cheese Stuffed Peppers

WEEK 12	MONDAY	TUESDAY	WEDNESDAY	THURSDAY	FRIDAY	SATURDAY	SUNDAY
MEAL 1	Mexican Pork Carnitas	Sausage & Veggie Muffins	Champions Breakfast Hash	Salmon with Asparagus	Tuscan Lamb Chops	Beef & Cheese Stuffed Peppers	Mexican Pork Carnitas
MEAL 2	Tuscan Lamb Chops	Rotisserie Chicken	Beef & Cheese Stuffed Peppers	Sausage & Veggie Muffins	Salmon with Asparagus	Mexican Pork Carnitas	Sausage & Veggie Muffins
MEAL 3	Salmon with Asparagus	Beef & Cheese Stuffed Peppers	Tuscan Lamb Chops	Rotisserie Chicken	Champions Breakfast Hash	Sausage & Veggie Muffins	Mexican Pork Carnitas

WEEK 13	MONDAY	TUESDAY	WEDNESDAY	THURSDAY	FRIDAY	SATURDAY	SUNDAY
MEAL 1	Beef & Cheese Stuffed Peppers	Champions Breakfast Hash	Mexican Pork Carnitas	Salmon with Asparagus	Tuscan Lamb Chops	Rotisserie Chicken	Sausage & Veggie Muffins
MEAL 2	Champions Breakfast Hash	Salmon with Asparagus	Beef & Cheese Stuffed Peppers	Tuscan Lamb Chops	Sausage & Veggie Muffins	Mexican Pork Carnitas	Rotisserie Chicken
MEAL 3	Sweet & Sticky Chicken	Asian Pork Chops	Spicy roasted chicken	Turkey with Spinach and Mushrooms	Citrus Creamy Fish	Spinach Mushroom Frittata	Tijuana Chili Beef

WEEK 14	MONDAY	TUESDAY	WEDNESDAY	THURSDAY	FRIDAY	SATURDAY	SUNDAY
MEAL 1	Turkey with Spinach and Mushrooms	Sweet & Sticky Chicken	Portuguese Shanks	Citrus Creamy Fish	Asian Pork Chops	Tijuana Chili Beef	Spinach Mushroom Frittata
MEAL 2	Asian Pork Chops	Spinach Mushroom Frittata	Tijuana Chili Beef	British Lamb Ribs	Citrus Creamy Fish	Turkey with Spinach and Mushrooms	Citrus Creamy Fish
MEAL 3	Citrus Creamy Fish	Japanese Balsamic Pork Roast	Asian Pork Chops	Tijuana Chili Beef	Spinach Mushroom Frittata	Sweet & Sticky Chicken	Tijuana Chili Beef

WEEK 15	MONDAY	TUESDAY	WEDNESDAY	THURSDAY	FRIDAY	SATURDAY	SUNDAY
MEAL 1	Tijuana Chili Beef	Sweet & Sticky Chicken	Citrus Creamy Fish	Asian Pork Chops	Turkey with Spinach and Mushrooms	Tuna Confit Salad	Spinach Mushroom Frittata
MEAL 2	Spinach Mushroom Frittata	Citrus Creamy Fish	Tijuana Chili Beef	Turkey with Spinach and Mushrooms	Popeye Frittata	Asian Pork Chops	Sweet & Sticky Chicken
MEAL 3	Worcestershire Chicken Salad	Cheesy Turkey with Mushrooms	Ultimate Breakfast Platter	Parma Lemon Fish	Creamy Chili with Beef	Hungarian beef goulash	Smoked Salmon Avocado Stuffing

WEEK 16	MONDAY	TUESDAY	WEDNESDAY	THURSDAY	FRIDAY	SATURDAY	SUNDAY
MEAL 1	Cheesy Turkey with Mushrooms	Ultimate Breakfast Platter	Creamy Chili with Beef	Hungarian beef goulash	Citrus Creamy Fish	Parma Lemon Fish	Creamy Chili with Beef
MEAL 2	Ultimate Breakfast Platter	Cheesy Turkey with Mushrooms	Spinach Mushroom Frittata	Creamy Chili with Beef	Parma Lemon Fish	Hungarian beef goulash	British Lamb Ribs
MEAL 3	Parma Lemon Fish	Ultimate Breakfast Platter	Creamy Chili with Beef	Cheesy Turkey with Mushrooms	Hungarian beef goulash	Tijuana Chili Beef	Rotisserie Chicken

WEEK 17	MONDAY	TUESDAY	WEDNESDAY	THURSDAY	FRIDAY	SATURDAY	SUNDAY
MEAL 1	Creamy Chili with Beef	Hungarian beef goulash	Ultimate Breakfast Platter	Parma Lemon Fish	Spinach Mushroom Frittata	Turkey Meatballs	Creamy Chili with Beef
MEAL 2	Hungarian beef goulash	Parma Lemon Fish	Cheesy Turkey with Mushrooms	Ultimate Breakfast Platter	Japanese Balsamic Pork Roast	Creamy Chili with Beef	Vegetarian Lasagna
MEAL 3	Chili Chicken Rice	Champions Low-Carb Breakfast	Instant Beef Steaks	Giant Pancake	Asian Pork Chops	Cheesy Turkey with Mushrooms	Mexican Pork Carnitas

WEEK 18	MONDAY	TUESDAY	WEDNESDAY	THURSDAY	FRIDAY	SATURDAY	SUNDAY
MEAL 1	Champions Low-Carb Breakfast	Instant Beef Steaks	Chili Chicken Rice	Vegetarian Lasagna	Parma Lemon Fish	Giant Pancake	Creamy Italian Chicken
MEAL 2	Instant Beef Steaks	Chili Chicken Rice	Vegetarian Lasagna	Giant Pancake	Winter Lamb Stew	Champions Low-Carb Breakfast	Sausage & Veggie Muffins
MEAL 3	Giant Pancake	Champions Low-Carb Breakfast	Chili Chicken Rice	Instant Beef Steaks	British Lamb Ribs	Salmon with Asparagus	Ultimate Breakfast Platter

WEEK 19	MONDAY	TUESDAY	WEDNESDAY	THURSDAY	FRIDAY	SATURDAY	SUNDAY
MEAL 1	Cauliflower Chicken Rice	Instant Pizza	Garlic Beef Steaks	Cottage Berry Pancake	Sausage & Veggie Muffins	Creamy Chili with Beef	Tijuana Chili Beef
MEAL 2	Instant Pizza	Cottage Berry Pancake	Cauliflower Chicken Rice	Garlic Beef Steaks	Giant Pancake	Instant Beef Steaks	Hungarian beef goulash
MEAL 3	Garlic Beef Steaks	Parma Lemon Fish	Tuscan Lamb Chops	Rotisserie Chicken	Beef & Cheese Stuffed Peppers	Champions Breakfast Hash	Cottage Berry Pancake

WEEK 20	MONDAY	TUESDAY	WEDNESDAY	THURSDAY	FRIDAY	SATURDAY	SUNDAY
MEAL 1	Cottage Berry Pancake	Garlic Beef Steaks	Rotisserie Chicken	Mexican Pork Carnitas	Garlic Beef Steaks	Salmon with Asparagus	Tuscan Lamb Chops
MEAL 2	Instant Carrot Chicken Pie	Carrot & Potato Soup	Beef & Cheese Stuffed Peppers	Salmon with Asparagus	Beef & Cheese Stuffed Peppers	Sausage & Veggie Muffins	Champions Breakfast Hash
MEAL 3	Carrot & Potato Soup	Instant Carrot Chicken Pie	Winter Lamb Stew	Vegetarian Lasagna	Turkey Meatballs	Beef-Stuffed Peppers	Creamy Italian Chicken

WEEK 21	MONDAY	TUESDAY	WEDNESDAY	THURSDAY	FRIDAY	SATURDAY	SUNDAY
MEAL 1	Creamy Chicken Pie	Broccoli Soup	Turkey Meatballs	Japanese Balsamic Pork Roast	Winter Lamb Stew	Vegetarian Lasagna	Coconut Fish Curry
MEAL 2	Broccoli Soup	Tijuana Chili Beef	Creamy Chicken Pie	Spinach Mushroom Frittata	Turkey with Spinach and Mushrooms	Asian Pork Chops	Sweet & Sticky Chicken
MEAL 3	Spicy roasted chicken	Spinach Mushroom Frittata	Beef meatballs in Marinara Sauce	Turkey with Spinach and Mushrooms	Bacon-Stuffed Avocados	Tuscan Lamb Chops	Tuna Confit Salad

WEEK 22	MONDAY	TUESDAY	WEDNESDAY	THURSDAY	FRIDAY	SATURDAY	SUNDAY
MEAL 1	Balsamic Turkey Meatballs	Worcestershire Chicken Salad	Japanese Balsamic Pork Roast	Portuguese Shanks	Tijuana Chili Beef	Creamy Pasta	Champions Breakfast Hash
MEAL 2	Bacon-Stuffed Avocados	Champions Breakfast Hash	Cheesy Turkey with Mushrooms	Instant Carrot Chicken Pie	Parma Lemon Fish	Lemongrass braised chicken	Lamb Chops in Masala Sauce
MEAL 3	Winter Lamb Stew	Spicy roasted chicken	Cauliflower and Broccoli Bake	Garlic Beef Steaks	Smoked Salmon Avocado Stuffing	Instant Pizza	Popeye Frittata

WEEK 23	MONDAY	TUESDAY	WEDNESDAY	THURSDAY	FRIDAY	SATURDAY	SUNDAY
MEAL 1	Salmon with Asparagus	Lemongrass braised chicken	Spicy roasted chicken	Creamy Pasta	Cheesy Turkey with Mushrooms	Garlic Beef Steaks	Salmon with Asparagus
MEAL 2	Tijuana Chili Beef	Broccoli Soup	Carrot & Potato Soup	Spicy roasted chicken	Beef-Stuffed Peppers	Citrus Creamy Fish	Champions Low-Carb Breakfast
MEAL 3	Hungarian beef goulash	Beef & Cheese Stuffed Peppers	Broccoli Soup	Creamy Chili with Beef	Spicy roasted chicken	Beef meatballs in Marinara Sauce	Turkey with Spinach and Mushrooms

WEEK 24	MONDAY	TUESDAY	WEDNESDAY	THURSDAY	FRIDAY	SATURDAY	SUNDAY
MEAL 1	Hainanese Chicken	Champions Low-Carb Breakfast	Cheesy Turkey with Mushrooms	Broccoli Soup	Parma Lemon Fish	Spicy roasted chicken	Instant Carrot Chicken Pie
MEAL 2	American Barbecue Turkey	Broccoli Soup	Portuguese Shanks	Creamy Pasta	Broccoli Soup	Carrot & Potato Soup	Spicy roasted chicken
MEAL 3	Japanese Balsamic Pork Roast	Creamy Chicken Pie	Creamy Pasta	Tijuana Chili Beef	Carrot & Potato Soup	Spicy roasted chicken	Japanese Balsamic Pork Roast

WEEK 25	MONDAY	TUESDAY	WEDNESDAY	THURSDAY	FRIDAY	SATURDAY	SUNDAY
MEAL 1	Tuscan Lamb Chops	Portuguese Shanks	Salmon with Asparagus	Carrot & Potato Soup	Spicy roasted chicken	Broccoli Soup	Beef meatballs in Marinara Sauce
MEAL 2	Citrus Creamy Fish	Sausage & Veggie Muffins	Worcestershire Chicken Salad	Spicy roasted chicken	Instant Pizza	Japanese Balsamic Pork Roast	Broccoli Soup
MEAL 3	Creamy Chili with Beef	Hainanese Chicken	Spicy roasted chicken	Tuscan Lamb Chops	Sausage & Veggie Muffins	Broccoli Soup	Cheesy Turkey with Mushrooms

WEEK 26	MONDAY	TUESDAY	WEDNESDAY	THURSDAY	FRIDAY	SATURDAY	SUNDAY
MEAL 1	Giant Pancake	Spicy roasted chicken	Carrot & Potato Soup	Creamy Chicken Pie	Broccoli Soup	Parma Lemon Fish	Carrot & Potato Soup
MEAL 2	Lemongrass braised chicken	Popeye Frittata	Turkey with Spinach and Mushrooms	Broccoli Soup	Cauliflower Chicken Rice	Cottage Berry Pancake	Garlic Beef Steaks
MEAL 3	Turkey Meatballs	Tuna Confit Salad	Broccoli Soup	British Lamb Ribs	Giant Pancake	Creamy Chicken Pie	Beef-Stuffed Peppers

WEEK 27	MONDAY	TUESDAY	WEDNESDAY	THURSDAY	FRIDAY	SATURDAY	SUNDAY
MEAL 1	Mexican Pork Carnitas	Broccoli Soup	Spicy roasted chicken	Carrot & Potato Soup	Sweet & Sticky Chicken	Worcestershire Chicken Salad	Lemongrass braised chicken
MEAL 2	Citrus Creamy Fish	Spinach Mushroom Frittata	Creamy Italian Chicken	Spicy roasted chicken	British Lamb Ribs	Creamy Italian Chicken	Giant Pancake
MEAL 3	Creamy Chili with Beef	Rotisserie Chicken	Carrot & Potato Soup	Worcestershire Chicken Salad	Spicy roasted chicken	Sweet & Sticky Chicken	Hainanese Chicken

WEEK 28	MONDAY	TUESDAY	WEDNESDAY	THURSDAY	FRIDAY	SATURDAY	SUNDAY
MEAL 1	Cottage Berry Pancake	Instant Carrot Chicken Pie	Broccoli Soup	Portobello Turkey legs	Hainanese Chicken	Spicy roasted chicken	Lamb Chops in Masala Sauce
MEAL 2	Portobello Turkey legs	Creamy Italian Chicken	Turkey Meatballs	Broccoli Soup	Turkey with Spinach and Mushrooms	Popeye Frittata	Spicy roasted chicken
MEAL 3	Popeye Frittata	Creamy Pasta	Sweet & Sticky Chicken	Rotisserie Chicken	Broccoli Soup	Carrot & Potato Soup	Turkey with Spinach and Mushrooms

WEEK 29	MONDAY	TUESDAY	WEDNESDAY	THURSDAY	FRIDAY	SATURDAY	SUNDAY
MEAL 1	Lamb Chops in Masala Sauce	Cauliflower Chicken Rice	Popeye Frittata	Hainanese Chicken	British Lamb Ribs	Lemongrass braised chicken	Portobello Turkey legs
MEAL 2	Tilapia and shrimp paella	Hainanese Chicken	Hainanese Chicken	British Lamb Ribs	Cheesy Turkey with Mushrooms	Giant Pancake	British Lamb Ribs
MEAL 3	Sommerset Meatza	Instant Pizza	British Lamb Ribs	Carrot & Potato Soup	Lemongrass braised chicken	Broccoli Soup	Winter Lamb Stew

WEEK 30	MONDAY	TUESDAY	WEDNESDAY	THURSDAY	FRIDAY	SATURDAY	SUNDAY
MEAL 1	Champions Breakfast Hash	Spinach Mushroom Frittata	Instant Pizza	Balsamic Turkey Meatballs	Giant Pancake	Cauliflower Chicken Rice	Broccoli Soup
MEAL 2	Asian Pork Chops	Balsamic Turkey Meatballs	Cauliflower Chicken Rice	Instant Pizza	Instant Carrot Chicken Pie	Turkey Meatballs	Balsamic Turkey Meatballs
MEAL 3	British Lamb Ribs	British Lamb Ribs	Bacon-Stuffed Avocados	Japanese Balsamic Pork Roast	Mexican Pork Carnitas	Broccoli Soup	Tilapia and shrimp paella

WEEK 31	MONDAY	TUESDAY	WEDNESDAY	THURSDAY	FRIDAY	SATURDAY	SUNDAY
MEAL 1	Smoked Salmon Avocado Stuffing	Cheesy Turkey with Mushrooms	Giant Pancake	Spinach Mushroom Frittata	Instant Pizza	Lamb Chops in Masala Sauce	Ultimate Breakfast Platter
MEAL 2	Beef-Stuffed Peppers	Carrot & Potato Soup	Asian Pork Chops	Bacon-Stuffed Avocados	Broccoli Soup	Portobello Turkey legs	Salmon with Asparagus
MEAL 3	Broccoli Soup	Bacon-Stuffed Avocados	Hainanese Chicken	Instant Carrot Chicken Pie	Balsamic Turkey Meatballs	Instant Pizza	Instant Carrot Chicken Pie

WEEK 32	MONDAY	TUESDAY	WEDNESDAY	THURSDAY	FRIDAY	SATURDAY	SUNDAY
MEAL 1	Carrot & Potato Soup	Creamy Italian Chicken	British Lamb Ribs	Broccoli Soup	Spinach Mushroom Frittata	Bacon-Stuffed Avocados	Citrus Creamy Fish
MEAL 2	Chili Chicken Rice	Giant Pancake	Sommerset Meatza	Sweet & Sticky Chicken	Turkey Meatballs	British Lamb Ribs	Instant Pizza
MEAL 3	Instant Beef Steaks	Broccoli Soup	Winter Lamb Stew	Cheesy Turkey with Mushrooms	Creamy Italian Chicken	Tuscan Lamb Chops	Parma Lemon Fish

WEEK 33	MONDAY	TUESDAY	WEDNESDAY	THURSDAY	FRIDAY	SATURDAY	SUNDAY
MEAL 1	American Barbecue Turkey	Winter Lamb Stew	Spinach Mushroom Frittata	Carrot & Potato Soup	Lemongrass braised chicken	Instant Pizza	Beef meatballs in Marinara Sauce
MEAL 2	Coconut Fish Curry	Sweet & Sticky Chicken	Lemongrass braised chicken	British Lamb Ribs	Carrot & Potato Soup	Portuguese Shanks	Sommerset Meatza
MEAL 3	Bacon-Stuffed Avocados	Spicy roasted chicken	Hainanese Chicken	Instant Pizza	Popeye Frittata	Carrot & Potato Soup	Creamy Chicken Pie

WEEK 34	MONDAY	TUESDAY	WEDNESDAY	THURSDAY	FRIDAY	SATURDAY	SUNDAY
MEAL 1	British Lamb Ribs	Worcestershire Chicken Salad	Instant Pizza	Turkey Meatballs	Carrot & Potato Soup	Creamy Chicken Pie	Worcestershire Chicken Salad
MEAL 2	Ultimate Breakfast Platter	Instant Pizza	Popeye Frittata	Hainanese Chicken	Creamy Chicken Pie	Creamy Italian Chicken	British Lamb Ribs
MEAL 3	Instant Carrot Chicken Pie	Lamb Chops in Masala Sauce	Carrot & Potato Soup	Creamy Chicken Pie	Bacon-Stuffed Avocados	Turkey with Spinach and Mushrooms	Popeye Frittata

WEEK 35	MONDAY	TUESDAY	WEDNESDAY	THURSDAY	FRIDAY	SATURDAY	SUNDAY
MEAL 1	Sausage & Veggie Muffins	Tilapia and shrimp paella	Creamy Chicken Pie	Carrot & Potato Soup	Asian Pork Chops	Balsamic Turkey Meatballs	Portuguese Shanks
MEAL 2	Instant Pizza	Creamy Chicken Pie	Rotisserie Chicken	Asian Pork Chops	Carrot & Potato Soup	British Lamb Ribs	Creamy Chili with Beef
MEAL 3	Winter Lamb Stew	Coconut Fish Curry	Creamy Chicken Pie	Spinach Mushroom Frittata	Coconut Fish Curry	Citrus Creamy Fish	Creamy Italian Chicken

WEEK 36	MONDAY	TUESDAY	WEDNESDAY	THURSDAY	FRIDAY	SATURDAY	SUNDAY
MEAL 1	Lebanese Zucchini Shakshuka	Chili Chicken Rice	Spicy roasted chicken	Creamy Chicken Pie	Salmon with Asparagus	Rotisserie Chicken	Instant Beef Steaks
MEAL 2	Tijuana Chili Beef	Turkey Meatballs	Smoked Salmon Avocado Stuffing	Smoked Salmon Avocado Stuffing	Creamy Chicken Pie	Portobello Turkey legs	Cheesy Turkey with Mushrooms
MEAL 3	Tuna Confit Salad	British Lamb Ribs	Mexican Pork Carnitas	Coconut Fish Curry	Worcestershire Chicken Salad	Creamy Chicken Pie	Spinach Mushroom Frittata

WEEK 37	MONDAY	TUESDAY	WEDNESDAY	THURSDAY	FRIDAY	SATURDAY	SUNDAY
MEAL 1	British Lamb Ribs	Smoked Salmon Avocado Stuffing	Tuna Confit Salad	Champions Low-Carb Breakfast	Spicy roasted chicken	Tilapia and shrimp paella	Creamy Chicken Pie
MEAL 2	Champions Low-Carb Breakfast	Lemongrass braised chicken	Chili Chicken Rice	Winter Lamb Stew	Sausage & Veggie Muffins	Creamy Chicken Pie	Asian Pork Chops
MEAL 3	Turkey with Spinach and Mushrooms	Sausage & Veggie Muffins	Coconut Fish Curry	Lemongrass braised chicken	Creamy Chicken Pie	Sausage & Veggie Muffins	Chili Chicken Rice

WEEK 38	MONDAY	TUESDAY	WEDNESDAY	THURSDAY	FRIDAY	SATURDAY	SUNDAY
MEAL 1	Creamy Italian Chicken	British Lamb Ribs	Lamb Chops in Masala Sauce	Tuscan Lamb Chops	Lamb Chops in Masala Sauce	Cheesy Turkey with Mushrooms	Creamy Italian Chicken
MEAL 2	Cheesy Turkey with Mushrooms	Salmon with Asparagus	Cheesy Turkey with Mushrooms	Parma Lemon Fish	Japanese Balsamic Pork Roast	Coconut Fish Curry	Beef-Stuffed Peppers
MEAL 3	Asian Pork Chops	Champions Low-Carb Breakfast	Sausage & Veggie Muffins	British Lamb Ribs	Smoked Salmon Avocado Stuffing	Cauliflower Chicken Rice	Tuscan Lamb Chops

WEEK 39	MONDAY	TUESDAY	WEDNESDAY	THURSDAY	FRIDAY	SATURDAY	SUNDAY
MEAL 1	Salmon with Asparagus	Citrus Creamy Fish	Citrus Creamy Fish	Hungarian beef goulash	Tuscan Lamb Chops	Japanese Balsamic Pork Roast	Creamy Pasta
MEAL 2	Hungarian beef goulash	Creamy Chicken Pie	Tuscan Lamb Chops	Cauliflower Chicken Rice	Cauliflower Chicken Rice	Beef meatballs in Marinara Sauce	Rotisserie Chicken
MEAL 3	Vegetarian Lasagna	Sommerset Meatza	Creamy Chicken Pie	Citrus Creamy Fish	Rotisserie Chicken	Hainanese Chicken	Spicy roasted chicken

WEEK 40	MONDAY	TUESDAY	WEDNESDAY	THURSDAY	FRIDAY	SATURDAY	SUNDAY
MEAL 1	Worcestershire Chicken Salad	Asian Pork Chops	Sommerset Meatza	Creamy Chicken Pie	Champions Low-Carb Breakfast	Asian Pork Chops	Garlic Beef Steaks
MEAL 2	American Barbecue Turkey	Turkey with Spinach and Mushrooms	Champions Low-Carb Breakfast	Turkey with Spinach and Mushrooms	Sweet & Sticky Chicken	Creamy Chili with Beef	Cauliflower and Broccoli Bake
MEAL 3	Mexican Pork Carnitas	Portuguese Shanks	Portobello Turkey legs	Turkey Meatballs	Portobello Turkey legs	British Lamb Ribs	Bacon-Stuffed Avocados

WEEK 41	MONDAY	TUESDAY	WEDNESDAY	THURSDAY	FRIDAY	SATURDAY	SUNDAY
MEAL 1	Turkey Meatballs	Lemongrass braised chicken	Sweet & Sticky Chicken	Popeye Frittata	Creamy Chicken Pie	Vegetarian Lasagna	Hungarian beef goulash
MEAL 2	Sweet & Sticky Chicken	Tuna Confit Salad	Hainanese Chicken	Tuna Confit Salad	Hainanese Chicken	Creamy Chicken Pie	Cauliflower and Broccoli Bake
MEAL 3	Sausage & Veggie Muffins	Garlic Beef Steaks	Tilapia and shrimp paella	Sausage & Veggie Muffins	Turkey Meatballs	Spicy roasted chicken	Champions Low-Carb Breakfast

WEEK 42	MONDAY	TUESDAY	WEDNESDAY	THURSDAY	FRIDAY	SATURDAY	SUNDAY
MEAL 1	Hungarian beef goulash	Balsamic Turkey Meatballs	Portuguese Shanks	Salmon with Asparagus	Creamy Italian Chicken	Instant Carrot Chicken Pie	Creamy Pasta
MEAL 2	Balsamic Turkey Meatballs	Worcestershire Chicken Salad	Spinach Mushroom Frittata	Lamb Chops in Masala Sauce	Tilapia and shrimp paella	Winter Lamb Stew	Lebanese Zucchini Shakshuka
MEAL 3	Pork Roast in Honey and garlic	Creamy Italian Chicken	British Lamb Ribs	Creamy Italian Chicken	Creamy Chicken Pie	Hungarian beef goulash	Tuna Confit Salad

WEEK 43	MONDAY	TUESDAY	WEDNESDAY	THURSDAY	FRIDAY	SATURDAY	SUNDAY
MEAL 1	Coconut Fish Curry	Spinach Mushroom Frittata	Japanese Balsamic Pork Roast	Creamy Chicken Pie	Lemongrass braised chicken	Ultimate Breakfast Platter	Turkey Meatballs
MEAL 2	Broccoli Soup	Beef meatballs in Marinara Sauce	Ultimate Breakfast Platter	Rotisserie Chicken	Ultimate Breakfast Platter	Sommerset Meatza	Lebanese Zucchini Shakshuka
MEAL 3	Instant Carrot Chicken Pie	Japanese Balsamic Pork Roast	Salmon with Asparagus	Hainanese Chicken	Spinach Mushroom Frittata	Champions Low-Carb Breakfast	Creamy Chicken Pie

WEEK 44	MONDAY	TUESDAY	WEDNESDAY	THURSDAY	FRIDAY	SATURDAY	SUNDAY
MEAL 1	Cottage Berry Pancake	Tilapia and shrimp paella	Coconut Fish Curry	Cheesy Turkey with Mushrooms	Coconut Fish Curry	Parma Lemon Fish	Creamy Chili with Beef
MEAL 2	Beef meatballs in Marinara Sauce	Tuscan Lamb Chops	Turkey with Spinach and Mushrooms	Tilapia and shrimp paella	Balsamic Turkey Meatballs	Sweet & Sticky Chicken	Vegetarian Lasagna
MEAL 3	Beef-Stuffed Peppers	Instant Carrot Chicken Pie	Creamy Chicken Pie	Asian Pork Chops	Winter Lamb Stew	Beef-Stuffed Peppers	Beef-Stuffed Peppers

WEEK 45	MONDAY	TUESDAY	WEDNESDAY	THURSDAY	FRIDAY	SATURDAY	SUNDAY
MEAL 1	Instant Carrot Chicken Pie	Portobello Turkey legs	Chili Chicken Rice	Worcestershire Chicken Salad	Chili Chicken Rice	Asian Pork Chops	Sommerset Meatza
MEAL 2	Creamy Chicken Pie	Ultimate Breakfast Platter	Beef meatballs in Marinara Sauce	Japanese Balsamic Pork Roast	Citrus Creamy Fish	Smoked Salmon Avocado Stuffing	Mexican Pork Carnitas
MEAL 3	Creamy Italian Chicken	Mexican Pork Carnitas	Asian Pork Chops	Mexican Pork Carnitas	Bacon-Stuffed Avocados	Instant Beef Steaks	Smoked Salmon Avocado Stuffing

WEEK 46	MONDAY	TUESDAY	WEDNESDAY	THURSDAY	FRIDAY	SATURDAY	SUNDAY
MEAL 1	Tilapia and shrimp paella	Creamy Chicken Pie	Creamy Italian Chicken	Popeye Frittata	Portuguese Shanks	Bacon-Stuffed Avocados	Hungarian beef goulash
MEAL 2	Ultimate Breakfast Platter	Chili Chicken Rice	Balsamic Turkey Meatballs	Turkey Meatballs	Parma Lemon Fish	Creamy Pasta	Japanese Balsamic Pork Roast
MEAL 3	Tuscan Lamb Chops	Rotisserie Chicken	Vegetarian Lasagna	Instant Carrot Chicken Pie	British Lamb Ribs	Creamy Chili with Beef	Sausage & Veggie Muffins

WEEK 47	MONDAY	TUESDAY	WEDNESDAY	THURSDAY	FRIDAY	SATURDAY	SUNDAY
MEAL 1	Cauliflower Chicken Rice	Hainanese Chicken	Lemongrass braised chicken	Creamy Chicken Pie	Cheesy Turkey with Mushrooms	Bacon-Stuffed Avocados	Sweet & Sticky Chicken
MEAL 2	Giant Pancake	Turkey Meatballs	Hungarian beef goulash	Portobello Turkey legs	British Lamb Ribs	Instant Beef Steaks	Garlic Beef Steaks
MEAL 3	Beef meatballs in Marinara Sauce	Portobello Turkey legs	Spicy roasted chicken	Lebanese Zucchini Shakshuka	Pork Roast in Honey and garlic	Tilapia and shrimp paella	Tuna Confit Salad

WEEK 48	MONDAY	TUESDAY	WEDNESDAY	THURSDAY	FRIDAY	SATURDAY	SUNDAY
MEAL 1	American Barbecue Turkey	Broccoli Soup	Portuguese Shanks	Broccoli Soup	Vegetarian Lasagna	Carrot & Potato Soup	Creamy Italian Chicken
MEAL 2	Instant Beef Steaks	Creamy Pasta	Winter Lamb Stew	Cheesy Turkey with Mushrooms	Creamy Italian Chicken	Tuscan Lamb Chops	Parma Lemon Fish
MEAL 3	Ultimate Breakfast Platter	Instant Pizza	Popeye Frittata	Instant Carrot Chicken Pie	Creamy Chicken Pie	Hainanese Chicken	British Lamb Ribs

WEEK 49	MONDAY	TUESDAY	WEDNESDAY	THURSDAY	FRIDAY	SATURDAY	SUNDAY
MEAL 1	Instant Carrot Chicken Pie	Chili Chicken Rice	Creamy Italian Chicken	Hungarian beef goulash	Japanese Balsamic Pork Roast	Coconut Fish Curry	Creamy Chili with Beef
MEAL 2	Salmon with Asparagus	Sommerset Meatza	Creamy Pasta	Chili Chicken Rice	Portobello Turkey legs	Spicy roasted chicken	Lebanese Zucchini Shakshuka
MEAL 3	Creamy Chicken Pie	Champions Low-Carb Breakfast	Lebanese Zucchini Shakshuka	Vegetarian Lasagna	Lamb Chops in Masala Sauce	Portobello Turkey legs	Beef meatballs in Marinara Sauce

WEEK 50	MONDAY	TUESDAY	WEDNESDAY	THURSDAY	FRIDAY	SATURDAY	SUNDAY
MEAL 1	Worcestershire Chicken Salad	Portobello Turkey legs	Tuna Confit Salad	Chili Chicken Rice	Hungarian beef goulash	Pork Roast in Honey and garlic	Lebanese Zucchini Shakshuka
MEAL 2	Spicy roasted chicken	Sweet & Sticky Chicken	Turkey Meatballs	Garlic Beef Steaks	Tuna Confit Salad	Tuna Confit Salad	Tilapia and shrimp paella
MEAL 3	Sausage & Veggie Muffins	Hainanese Chicken	Lebanese Zucchini Shakshuka	Cauliflower Chicken Rice	Balsamic Turkey Meatballs	Tilapia and shrimp paella	Lebanese Zucchini Shakshuka

WEEK 51	MONDAY	TUESDAY	WEDNESDAY	THURSDAY	FRIDAY	SATURDAY	SUNDAY
MEAL 1	Creamy Chicken Pie	Tilapia and shrimp paella	Creamy Chicken Pie	Tuscan Lamb Chops	Popeye Frittata	Sausage & Veggie Muffins	Sausage & Veggie Muffins
MEAL 2	Vegetarian Lasagna	Portuguese Shanks	Creamy Chili with Beef	Rotisserie Chicken	Cauliflower and Broccoli Bake	Lebanese Zucchini Shakshuka	Beef meatballs in Marinara Sauce
MEAL 3	Lamb Chops in Masala Sauce	Spinach Mushroom Frittata	Vegetarian Lasagna	Beef & Cheese Stuffed Peppers	Hainanese Chicken	Hainanese Chicken	Balsamic Turkey Meatballs

WEEK 52	MONDAY	TUESDAY	WEDNESDAY	THURSDAY	FRIDAY	SATURDAY	SUNDAY
MEAL 1	Japanese Balsamic Pork Roast	British Lamb Ribs	Beef-Stuffed Peppers	Winter Lamb Stew	Creamy Pasta	Balsamic Turkey Meatballs	Hainanese Chicken
MEAL 2	Smoked Salmon Avocado Stuffing	Japanese Balsamic Pork Roast	Tilapia and shrimp paella	Lemongrass braised chicken	Beef & Cheese Stuffed Peppers	Beef meatballs in Marinara Sauce	Spicy roasted chicken
MEAL 3	Tuscan Lamb Chops	Ultimate Breakfast Platter	Creamy Chicken Pie	Turkey Meatballs	Cauliflower Chicken Rice	Popeye Frittata	Balsamic Turkey Meatballs

WEEK 53	MONDAY	TUESDAY	WEDNESDAY	THURSDAY	FRIDAY	SATURDAY	SUNDAY
MEAL 1	Cauliflower Chicken Rice	Salmon with Asparagus	Coconut Fish Curry	Creamy Chicken Pie	American Barbecue Turkey	Lamb Chops in Masala Sauce	Cauliflower and Broccoli Bake
MEAL 2	Rotisserie Chicken	American Barbecue Turkey	Instant Beef Steaks	Beef meatballs in Marinara Sauce	Lemongrass braised chicken	Tuna Confit Salad	Hungarian beef goulash
MEAL 3	American Barbecue Turkey	Broccoli Soup	Lemongrass braised chicken	Lemongrass braised chicken	Cottage Berry Pancake	Beef meatballs in Marinara Sauce	Spicy roasted chicken

WEEK 54	MONDAY	TUESDAY	WEDNESDAY	THURSDAY	FRIDAY	SATURDAY	SUNDAY
MEAL 1	Tilapia and shrimp paella	Smoked Salmon Avocado Stuffing	Chili Chicken Rice	Carrot & Potato Soup	Portuguese Shanks	Bacon-Stuffed Avocados	Smoked Salmon Avocado Stuffing
MEAL 2	Creamy Chicken Pie	American Barbecue Turkey	Champions Low-Carb Breakfast	Japanese Balsamic Pork Roast	Spicy roasted chicken	Hungarian beef goulash	Tuna Confit Salad
MEAL 3	Coconut Fish Curry	Broccoli Soup	Beef-Stuffed Peppers	Cheesy Turkey with Mushrooms	Portobello Turkey legs	Cauliflower and Broccoli Bake	Popeye Frittata

WEEK 55	MONDAY	TUESDAY	WEDNESDAY	THURSDAY	FRIDAY	SATURDAY	SUNDAY
MEAL 1	Instant Beef Steaks	Beef & Cheese Stuffed Peppers	Instant Pizza	Cauliflower and Broccoli Bake	Spicy roasted chicken	Lemongrass braised chicken	Bacon-Stuffed Avocados
MEAL 2	Chili Chicken Rice	Coconut Fish Curry	Cottage Berry Pancake	Spicy roasted chicken	Lebanese Zucchini Shakshuka	American Barbecue Turkey	Cauliflower Chicken Rice
MEAL 3	Spicy roasted chicken	Winter Lamb Stew	Parma Lemon Fish	Carrot & Potato Soup	Parma Lemon Fish	American Barbecue Turkey	British Lamb Ribs

WEEK 56	MONDAY	TUESDAY	WEDNESDAY	THURSDAY	FRIDAY	SATURDAY	SUNDAY
MEAL 1	Lemongrass braised chicken	Broccoli Soup	Beef-Stuffed Peppers	Broccoli Soup	Spicy roasted chicken	Bacon-Stuffed Avocados	Smoked Salmon Avocado Stuffing
MEAL 2	Broccoli Soup	Turkey Meatballs	Garlic Beef Steaks	Cottage Berry Pancake	Tuna Confit Salad	British Lamb Ribs	Japanese Balsamic Pork Roast
MEAL 3	Beef & Cheese Stuffed Peppers	Creamy Italian Chicken	Carrot & Potato Soup	Creamy Chicken Pie	Cauliflower and Broccoli Bake	Parma Lemon Fish	Creamy Chicken Pie

WEEK 57	MONDAY	TUESDAY	WEDNESDAY	THURSDAY	FRIDAY	SATURDAY	SUNDAY
MEAL 1	Spinach Mushroom Frittata	Japanese Balsamic Pork Roast	Instant Carrot Chicken Pie	Rotisserie Chicken	Asian Pork Chops	Smoked Salmon Avocado Stuffing	Creamy Pasta
MEAL 2	Creamy Chicken Pie	Cauliflower Chicken Rice	Beef-Stuffed Peppers	Creamy Chicken Pie	Spinach Mushroom Frittata	Sommerset Meatza	American Barbecue Turkey
MEAL 3	Parma Lemon Fish	Winter Lamb Stew	Broccoli Soup	Cottage Berry Pancake	Cauliflower Chicken Rice	Creamy Pasta	Lemongrass braised chicken

WEEK 58	MONDAY	TUESDAY	WEDNESDAY	THURSDAY	FRIDAY	SATURDAY	SUNDAY
MEAL 1	Smoked Salmon Avocado Stuffing	Beef & Cheese Stuffed Peppers	Tijuana Chili Beef	Spicy roasted chicken	Creamy Chicken Pie	Spinach Mushroom Frittata	Spinach Mushroom Frittata
MEAL 2	Sommerset Meatza	Salmon with Asparagus	Spinach Mushroom Frittata	Smoked Salmon Avocado Stuffing	Smoked Salmon Avocado Stuffing	Creamy Italian Chicken	Winter Lamb Stew
MEAL 3	Creamy Pasta	Cauliflower Chicken Rice	Beef-Stuffed Peppers	Mexican Pork Carnitas	Coconut Fish Curry	Turkey Meatballs	Japanese Balsamic Pork Roast

WEEK 59	MONDAY	TUESDAY	WEDNESDAY	THURSDAY	FRIDAY	SATURDAY	SUNDAY
MEAL 1	Creamy Italian Chicken	Beef & Cheese Stuffed Peppers	Worcestershire Chicken Salad	Carrot & Potato Soup	Tuna Confit Salad	Japanese Balsamic Pork Roast	Turkey Meatballs
MEAL 2	Turkey Meatballs	Mexican Pork Carnitas	Champions Breakfast Hash	Tuna Confit Salad	Champions Low-Carb Breakfast	Tuna Confit Salad	Mexican Pork Carnitas
MEAL 3	Japanese Balsamic Pork Roast	Sausage & Veggie Muffins	Spicy roasted chicken	Chili Chicken Rice	Winter Lamb Stew	Winter Lamb Stew	Creamy Italian Chicken

WEEK 60	MONDAY	TUESDAY	WEDNESDAY	THURSDAY	FRIDAY	SATURDAY	SUNDAY
MEAL 1	Winter Lamb Stew	Cauliflower Chicken Rice	Beef-Stuffed Peppers	Coconut Fish Curry	Lemongrass braised chicken	Coconut Fish Curry	Winter Lamb Stew
MEAL 2	Salmon with Asparagus	Rotisserie Chicken	Lemongrass braised chicken	Salmon with Asparagus	Cauliflower Chicken Rice	Beef-Stuffed Peppers	Creamy Italian Chicken
MEAL 3	Worcestershire Chicken Salad	Mexican Pork Carnitas	Broccoli Soup	Lamb Chops in Masala Sauce	Tuscan Lamb Chops	Vegetarian Lasagna	Beef & Cheese Stuffed Peppers

WEEK 61	MONDAY	TUESDAY	WEDNESDAY	THURSDAY	FRIDAY	SATURDAY	SUNDAY
MEAL 1	Spicy roasted chicken	Spinach Mushroom Frittata	Beef & Cheese Stuffed Peppers	Cheesy Turkey with Mushrooms	Parma Lemon Fish	Vegetarian Lasagna	Coconut Fish Curry
MEAL 2	Carrot & Potato Soup	Creamy Chili with Beef	Giant Pancake	Sausage & Veggie Muffins	British Lamb Ribs	Rotisserie Chicken	Sausage & Veggie Muffins
MEAL 3	Turkey with Spinach and Mushrooms	British Lamb Ribs	Instant Carrot Chicken Pie	Salmon with Asparagus	Cauliflower Chicken Rice	Sausage & Veggie Muffins	Rotisserie Chicken

WEEK 62	MONDAY	TUESDAY	WEDNESDAY	THURSDAY	FRIDAY	SATURDAY	SUNDAY
MEAL 1	Broccoli Soup	Rotisserie Chicken	Mexican Pork Carnitas	Citrus Creamy Fish	Hungarian beef goulash	Champions Breakfast Hash	Sausage & Veggie Muffins
MEAL 2	Spicy roasted chicken	Creamy Chili with Beef	Instant Pizza	Tuscan Lamb Chops	Cauliflower Chicken Rice	Creamy Chili with Beef	Rotisserie Chicken
MEAL 3	Creamy Italian Chicken	Vegetarian Lasagna	Broccoli Soup	Creamy Chicken Pie	Citrus Creamy Fish	Tilapia and shrimp paella	Tijuana Chili Beef

WEEK 63	MONDAY	TUESDAY	WEDNESDAY	THURSDAY	FRIDAY	SATURDAY	SUNDAY
MEAL 1	Sausage & Veggie Muffins	Mexican Pork Carnitas	Balsamic Turkey Meatballs	Salmon with Asparagus	Salmon with Asparagus	Tilapia and shrimp paella	Spinach Mushroom Frittata
MEAL 2	Salmon with Asparagus	Creamy Italian Chicken	Cauliflower Chicken Rice	Sommerset Meatza	Creamy Chicken Pie	Pork Roast in Honey and garlic	Citrus Creamy Fish
MEAL 3	American Barbecue Turkey	Sausage & Veggie Muffins	Citrus Creamy Fish	Champions Low-Carb Breakfast	Turkey with Spinach and Mushrooms	Portuguese Shanks	Tijuana Chili Beef

WEEK 64	MONDAY	TUESDAY	WEDNESDAY	THURSDAY	FRIDAY	SATURDAY	SUNDAY
MEAL 1	Coconut Fish Curry	Creamy Chicken Pie	Spinach Mushroom Frittata	Coconut Fish Curry	Worcestershire Chicken Salad	Spicy roasted chicken	Spinach Mushroom Frittata
MEAL 2	American Barbecue Turkey	Cauliflower Chicken Rice	Coconut Fish Curry	Giant Pancake	Champions Breakfast Hash	Pork Roast in Honey and garlic	Sweet & Sticky Chicken
MEAL 3	Chili Chicken Rice	Spicy roasted chicken	Creamy Chicken Pie	Salmon with Asparagus	Spicy roasted chicken	Portuguese Shanks	Smoked Salmon Avocado Stuffing

WEEK 65	MONDAY	TUESDAY	WEDNESDAY	THURSDAY	FRIDAY	SATURDAY	SUNDAY
MEAL 1	Turkey Meatballs	Smoked Salmon Avocado Stuffing	Smoked Salmon Avocado Stuffing	Creamy Chicken Pie	Lemongrass braised chicken	Pork Roast in Honey and garlic	Creamy Chili with Beef
MEAL 2	British Lamb Ribs	Mexican Pork Carnitas	Coconut Fish Curry	Worcestershire Chicken Salad	Broccoli Soup	Hungarian beef goulash	British Lamb Ribs
MEAL 3	American Barbecue Turkey	Cauliflower Chicken Rice	Coconut Fish Curry	Giant Pancake	Beef & Cheese Stuffed Peppers	Tuna Confit Salad	Rotisserie Chicken

WEEK 66	MONDAY	TUESDAY	WEDNESDAY	THURSDAY	FRIDAY	SATURDAY	SUNDAY
MEAL 1	Smoked Salmon Avocado Stuffing	Tuna Confit Salad	Champions Low-Carb Breakfast	Spicy roasted chicken	Champions Low-Carb Breakfast	Hungarian beef goulash	Creamy Chili with Beef
MEAL 2	Lemongrass braised chicken	Chili Chicken Rice	Winter Lamb Stew	Sausage & Veggie Muffins	Broccoli Soup	Popeye Frittata	Vegetarian Lasagna
MEAL 3	Sausage & Veggie Muffins	Coconut Fish Curry	Lemongrass braised chicken	Creamy Chicken Pie	Creamy Chicken Pie	Hainanese Chicken	Mexican Pork Carnitas

WEEK 67	MONDAY	TUESDAY	WEDNESDAY	THURSDAY	FRIDAY	SATURDAY	SUNDAY
MEAL 1	Winter Lamb Stew	Cauliflower Chicken Rice	Champions Breakfast Hash	Asian Pork Chops	Portuguese Shanks	Lamb Chops in Masala Sauce	Creamy Italian Chicken
MEAL 2	British Lamb Ribs	Lamb Chops in Masala Sauce	Tuscan Lamb Chops	Lamb Chops in Masala Sauce	Sausage & Veggie Muffins	Tuna Confit Salad	Sausage & Veggie Muffins
MEAL 3	Salmon with Asparagus	Cheesy Turkey with Mushrooms	Parma Lemon Fish	Japanese Balsamic Pork Roast	Hainanese Chicken	Smoked Salmon Avocado Stuffing	Ultimate Breakfast Platter

WEEK 68	MONDAY	TUESDAY	WEDNESDAY	THURSDAY	FRIDAY	SATURDAY	SUNDAY
MEAL 1	Champions Low-Carb Breakfast	Sausage & Veggie Muffins	British Lamb Ribs	Smoked Salmon Avocado Stuffing	Spicy roasted chicken	Creamy Pasta	Tijuana Chili Beef
MEAL 2	Winter Lamb Stew	Lebanese Zucchini Shakshuka	Beef & Cheese Stuffed Peppers	Winter Lamb Stew	Popeye Frittata	Sommerset Meatza	Hungarian beef goulash
MEAL 3	Creamy Chicken Pie	Cauliflower Chicken Rice	Winter Lamb Stew	Coconut Fish Curry	Tuna Confit Salad	Bacon-Stuffed Avocados	Creamy Italian Chicken

WEEK 69	MONDAY	TUESDAY	WEDNESDAY	THURSDAY	FRIDAY	SATURDAY	SUNDAY
MEAL 1	Citrus Creamy Fish	Citrus Creamy Fish	Hungarian beef goulash	Tuscan Lamb Chops	Rotisserie Chicken	Bacon-Stuffed Avocados	Cottage Berry Pancake
MEAL 2	Creamy Chicken Pie	Tuscan Lamb Chops	Cauliflower Chicken Rice	Cauliflower Chicken Rice	Broccoli Soup	British Lamb Ribs	Tuscan Lamb Chops
MEAL 3	Sommerset Meatza	Creamy Chicken Pie	Citrus Creamy Fish	Rotisserie Chicken	Spinach Mushroom Frittata	Creamy Pasta	Champions Breakfast Hash

WEEK 70	MONDAY	TUESDAY	WEDNESDAY	THURSDAY	FRIDAY	SATURDAY	SUNDAY
MEAL 1	Asian Pork Chops	Sommerset Meatza	Creamy Chicken Pie	Champions Low-Carb Breakfast	Instant Carrot Chicken Pie	Mexican Pork Carnitas	Cheesy Turkey with Mushrooms
MEAL 2	Turkey with Spinach and Mushrooms	Champions Low-Carb Breakfast	Turkey with Spinach and Mushrooms	Sweet & Sticky Chicken	Creamy Italian Chicken	Vegetarian Lasagna	Carrot & Potato Soup
MEAL 3	Portuguese Shanks	Portobello Turkey legs	Turkey Meatballs	Portobello Turkey legs	Creamy Pasta	Beef-Stuffed Peppers	Bacon-Stuffed Avocados

92

WEEK 71	MONDAY	TUESDAY	WEDNESDAY	THURSDAY	FRIDAY	SATURDAY	SUNDAY
MEAL 1	Lemongrass braised chicken	Sweet & Sticky Chicken	Popeye Frittata	Creamy Chicken Pie	Cauliflower Chicken Rice	Coconut Fish Curry	British Lamb Ribs
MEAL 2	Tuna Confit Salad	Hainanese Chicken	Tuna Confit Salad	Hainanese Chicken	Hainanese Chicken	Beef-Stuffed Peppers	Sweet & Sticky Chicken
MEAL 3	Garlic Beef Steaks	Tilapia and shrimp paella	Sausage & Veggie Muffins	Turkey Meatballs	Instant Pizza	Winter Lamb Stew	Balsamic Turkey Meatballs

WEEK 72	MONDAY	TUESDAY	WEDNESDAY	THURSDAY	FRIDAY	SATURDAY	SUNDAY
MEAL 1	Balsamic Turkey Meatballs	Portuguese Shanks	Salmon with Asparagus	Creamy Italian Chicken	Spinach Mushroom Frittata	Ultimate Breakfast Platter	Winter Lamb Stew
MEAL 2	Worcestershire Chicken Salad	Spinach Mushroom Frittata	Lamb Chops in Masala Sauce	Tilapia and shrimp paella	Balsamic Turkey Meatballs	Salmon with Asparagus	Bacon-Stuffed Avocados
MEAL 3	Tilapia and shrimp paella	Tilapia and shrimp paella	Winter Lamb Stew	Creamy Italian Chicken	British Lamb Ribs	Instant Carrot Chicken Pie	Salmon with Asparagus

WEEK 73	MONDAY	TUESDAY	WEDNESDAY	THURSDAY	FRIDAY	SATURDAY	SUNDAY
MEAL 1	Portuguese Shanks	Spicy roasted chicken	Salmon with Asparagus	Beef & Cheese Stuffed Peppers	Cheesy Turkey with Mushrooms	Citrus Creamy Fish	Hungarian beef goulash
MEAL 2	Spinach Mushroom Frittata	Beef meatballs in Marinara Sauce	Mexican Pork Carnitas	Asian Pork Chops	Carrot & Potato Soup	Instant Pizza	Bacon-Stuffed Avocados
MEAL 3	British Lamb Ribs	Balsamic Turkey Meatballs	Beef & Cheese Stuffed Peppers	Mexican Pork Carnitas	Bacon-Stuffed Avocados	Parma Lemon Fish	Hainanese Chicken

WEEK 74	MONDAY	TUESDAY	WEDNESDAY	THURSDAY	FRIDAY	SATURDAY	SUNDAY
MEAL 1	Japanese Balsamic Pork Roast	Balsamic Turkey Meatballs	Sausage & Veggie Muffins	Mexican Pork Carnitas	British Lamb Ribs	Lamb Chops in Masala Sauce	Tuscan Lamb Chops
MEAL 2	Ultimate Breakfast Platter	Asian Pork Chops	Sausage & Veggie Muffins	Bacon-Stuffed Avocados	Sweet & Sticky Chicken	Worcestershire Chicken Salad	Japanese Balsamic Pork Roast
MEAL 3	Salmon with Asparagus	Cauliflower and Broccoli Bake	Rotisserie Chicken	Sausage & Veggie Muffins	Balsamic Turkey Meatballs	Parma Lemon Fish	Japanese Balsamic Pork Roast

WEEK 75	MONDAY	TUESDAY	WEDNESDAY	THURSDAY	FRIDAY	SATURDAY	SUNDAY
MEAL 1	American Barbecue Turkey	Spicy roasted chicken	Spinach Mushroom Frittata	Tijuana Chili Beef	Winter Lamb Stew	Spicy roasted chicken	Cauliflower and Broccoli Bake
MEAL 2	Smoked Salmon Avocado Stuffing	Sausage & Veggie Muffins	Mexican Pork Carnitas	Cauliflower and Broccoli Bake	Bacon-Stuffed Avocados	Parma Lemon Fish	Japanese Balsamic Pork Roast
MEAL 3	American Barbecue Turkey	Creamy Chicken Pie	Tijuana Chili Beef	Spinach Mushroom Frittata	Salmon with Asparagus	Lemongrass braised chicken	Spicy roasted chicken

WEEK 76	MONDAY	TUESDAY	WEDNESDAY	THURSDAY	FRIDAY	SATURDAY	SUNDAY
MEAL 1	Beef & Cheese Stuffed Peppers	Garlic Beef Steaks	Sweet & Sticky Chicken	Tijuana Chili Beef	Hungarian beef goulash	Beef & Cheese Stuffed Peppers	Champions Breakfast Hash
MEAL 2	Coconut Fish Curry	Carrot & Potato Soup	Asian Pork Chops	Cauliflower and Broccoli Bake	Bacon-Stuffed Avocados	Portuguese Shanks	Broccoli Soup
MEAL 3	Winter Lamb Stew	Instant Carrot Chicken Pie	Tuna Confit Salad	Spinach Mushroom Frittata	Hainanese Chicken	Worcestershire Chicken Salad	Spinach Mushroom Frittata

WEEK 77	MONDAY	TUESDAY	WEDNESDAY	THURSDAY	FRIDAY	SATURDAY	SUNDAY
MEAL 1	Turkey Meatballs	Tijuana Chili Beef	Hungarian beef goulash	Smoked Salmon Avocado Stuffing	Champions Low-Carb Breakfast	Creamy Chicken Pie	Creamy Pasta
MEAL 2	Creamy Italian Chicken	Spinach Mushroom Frittata	Vegetarian Lasagna	Sweet & Sticky Chicken	Japanese Balsamic Pork Roast	Broccoli Soup	Cheesy Turkey with Mushrooms
MEAL 3	Japanese Balsamic Pork Roast	Worcestershire Chicken Salad	Parma Lemon Fish	Creamy Chili with Beef	Lamb Chops in Masala Sauce	Tuscan Lamb Chops	Lamb Chops in Masala Sauce

WEEK 78	MONDAY	TUESDAY	WEDNESDAY	THURSDAY	FRIDAY	SATURDAY	SUNDAY
MEAL 1	Winter Lamb Stew	Spicy roasted chicken	Tijuana Chili Beef	Rotisserie Chicken	American Barbecue Turkey	Parma Lemon Fish	Japanese Balsamic Pork Roast
MEAL 2	Beef & Cheese Stuffed Peppers	Champions Breakfast Hash	Hungarian beef goulash	Salmon with Asparagus	Sausage & Veggie Muffins	British Lamb Ribs	Smoked Salmon Avocado Stuffing
MEAL 3	Salmon with Asparagus	Turkey with Spinach and Mushrooms	Turkey Meatballs	Creamy Chili with Beef	Cheesy Turkey with Mushrooms	Vegetarian Lasagna	Sweet & Sticky Chicken

WEEK 79	MONDAY	TUESDAY	WEDNESDAY	THURSDAY	FRIDAY	SATURDAY	SUNDAY
MEAL 1	Beef & Cheese Stuffed Peppers	Citrus Creamy Fish	Cheesy Turkey with Mushrooms	Mexican Pork Carnitas	Citrus Creamy Fish	Vegetarian Lasagna	Sweet & Sticky Chicken
MEAL 2	Mexican Pork Carnitas	Salmon with Asparagus	Creamy Chili with Beef	Creamy Chicken Pie	Cauliflower and Broccoli Bake	Hungarian beef goulash	Tuscan Lamb Chops
MEAL 3	Sausage & Veggie Muffins	Sausage & Veggie Muffins	Giant Pancake	Creamy Italian Chicken	Tuscan Lamb Chops	Cauliflower Chicken Rice	Cauliflower Chicken Rice

WEEK 80	MONDAY	TUESDAY	WEDNESDAY	THURSDAY	FRIDAY	SATURDAY	SUNDAY
MEAL 1	Rotisserie Chicken	Tuscan Lamb Chops	Salmon with Asparagus	Ultimate Breakfast Platter	Portobello Turkey legs	Champions Low-Carb Breakfast	Ultimate Breakfast Platter
MEAL 2	Mexican Pork Carnitas	Vegetarian Lasagna	Champions Low-Carb Breakfast	Sausage & Veggie Muffins	Sommerset Meatza	Creamy Chicken Pie	Rotisserie Chicken
MEAL 3	Spinach Mushroom Frittata	Asian Pork Chops	Creamy Chili with Beef	Tijuana Chili Beef	Champions Low-Carb Breakfast	Turkey with Spinach and Mushrooms	Sweet & Sticky Chicken

WEEK 81	MONDAY	TUESDAY	WEDNESDAY	THURSDAY	FRIDAY	SATURDAY	SUNDAY
MEAL 1	Tilapia and shrimp paella	Lebanese Zucchini Shakshuka	Instant Beef Steaks	Hungarian beef goulash	Tilapia and shrimp paella	Tuna Confit Salad	Hainanese Chicken
MEAL 2	Lebanese Zucchini Shakshuka	Beef meatballs in Marinara Sauce	Champions Breakfast Hash	Cottage Berry Pancake	Sweet & Sticky Chicken	Popeye Frittata	Creamy Chicken Pie
MEAL 3	Spicy roasted chicken	Portobello Turkey legs	Salmon with Asparagus	Tuscan Lamb Chops	Hainanese Chicken	Turkey Meatballs	Portobello Turkey legs

WEEK 82	MONDAY	TUESDAY	WEDNESDAY	THURSDAY	FRIDAY	SATURDAY	SUNDAY
MEAL 1	Beef meatballs in Marinara Sauce	Tilapia and shrimp paella	Sausage & Veggie Muffins	Champions Breakfast Hash	Tilapia and shrimp paella	Sausage & Veggie Muffins	Turkey Meatballs
MEAL 2	Balsamic Turkey Meatballs	Cauliflower and Broccoli Bake	Beef-Stuffed Peppers	Creamy Italian Chicken	Portuguese Shanks	Salmon with Asparagus	Creamy Italian Chicken
MEAL 3	Hainanese Chicken	Popeye Frittata	Champions Breakfast Hash	Spinach Mushroom Frittata	Tilapia and shrimp paella	Lamb Chops in Masala Sauce	Tilapia and shrimp paella

WEEK 83	MONDAY	TUESDAY	WEDNESDAY	THURSDAY	FRIDAY	SATURDAY	SUNDAY
MEAL 1	Balsamic Turkey Meatballs	Hainanese Chicken	Garlic Beef Steaks	Smoked Salmon Avocado Stuffing	Lebanese Zucchini Shakshuka	Beef & Cheese Stuffed Peppers	Champions Breakfast Hash
MEAL 2	Cauliflower and Broccoli Bake	Hungarian beef goulash	Carrot & Potato Soup	Beef-Stuffed Peppers	Spicy roasted chicken	Salmon with Asparagus	Beef & Cheese Stuffed Peppers
MEAL 3	Hungarian beef goulash	Cauliflower and Broccoli Bake	Instant Carrot Chicken Pie	Broccoli Soup	Beef meatballs in Marinara Sauce	Winter Lamb Stew	Creamy Italian Chicken

WEEK 84	MONDAY	TUESDAY	WEDNESDAY	THURSDAY	FRIDAY	SATURDAY	SUNDAY
MEAL 1	Tuna Confit Salad	Balsamic Turkey Meatballs	Tijuana Chili Beef	Carrot & Potato Soup	Hainanese Chicken	Mexican Pork Carnitas	Sausage & Veggie Muffins
MEAL 2	Popeye Frittata	Lamb Chops in Masala Sauce	Spinach Mushroom Frittata	Chili Chicken Rice	Balsamic Turkey Meatballs	Sausage & Veggie Muffins	Mexican Pork Carnitas
MEAL 3	Bacon-Stuffed Avocados	American Barbecue Turkey	Worcestershire Chicken Salad	Instant Beef Steaks	Cauliflower and Broccoli Bake	Beef & Cheese Stuffed Peppers	Mexican Pork Carnitas

WEEK 85	MONDAY	TUESDAY	WEDNESDAY	THURSDAY	FRIDAY	SATURDAY	SUNDAY
MEAL 1	British Lamb Ribs	Smoked Salmon Avocado Stuffing	Spicy roasted chicken	American Barbecue Turkey	Hungarian beef goulash	Mexican Pork Carnitas	Rotisserie Chicken
MEAL 2	Smoked Salmon Avocado Stuffing	American Barbecue Turkey	Tuscan Lamb Chops	Coconut Fish Curry	Spicy roasted chicken	Spinach Mushroom Frittata	Tijuana Chili Beef
MEAL 3	Japanese Balsamic Pork Roast	Smoked Salmon Avocado Stuffing	Salmon with Asparagus	Bacon-Stuffed Avocados	Sausage & Veggie Muffins	Rotisserie Chicken	Sausage & Veggie Muffins

WEEK 86	MONDAY	TUESDAY	WEDNESDAY	THURSDAY	FRIDAY	SATURDAY	SUNDAY
MEAL 1	Creamy Pasta	Lamb Chops in Masala Sauce	Citrus Creamy Fish	Balsamic Turkey Meatballs	Instant Carrot Chicken Pie	Tuna Confit Salad	Worcestershire Chicken Salad
MEAL 2	American Barbecue Turkey	Bacon-Stuffed Avocados	Tuscan Lamb Chops	Rotisserie Chicken	Garlic Beef Steaks	Sweet & Sticky Chicken	Tijuana Chili Beef
MEAL 3	Lemongrass braised chicken	Japanese Balsamic Pork Roast	Sausage & Veggie Muffins	Mexican Pork Carnitas	Carrot & Potato Soup	American Barbecue Turkey	American Barbecue Turkey

WEEK 87	MONDAY	TUESDAY	WEDNESDAY	THURSDAY	FRIDAY	SATURDAY	SUNDAY
MEAL 1	Winter Lamb Stew	Turkey Meatballs	Spinach Mushroom Frittata	Spinach Mushroom Frittata	Broccoli Soup	Asian Pork Chops	Sweet & Sticky Chicken
MEAL 2	Japanese Balsamic Pork Roast	Creamy Italian Chicken	Asian Pork Chops	Tijuana Chili Beef	Tijuana Chili Beef	Hungarian beef goulash	Smoked Salmon Avocado Stuffing
MEAL 3	Turkey Meatballs	Coconut Fish Curry	Citrus Creamy Fish	Turkey with Spinach and Mushrooms	Spinach Mushroom Frittata	American Barbecue Turkey	Spinach Mushroom Frittata

WEEK 88	MONDAY	TUESDAY	WEDNESDAY	THURSDAY	FRIDAY	SATURDAY	SUNDAY
MEAL 1	Creamy Italian Chicken	Japanese Balsamic Pork Roast	Champions Breakfast Hash	Sweet & Sticky Chicken	Worcestershire Chicken Salad	Hungarian beef goulash	British Lamb Ribs
MEAL 2	Winter Lamb Stew	Vegetarian Lasagna	Turkey with Spinach and Mushrooms	Tuna Confit Salad	Spicy roasted chicken	Tijuana Chili Beef	Rotisserie Chicken
MEAL 3	Creamy Italian Chicken	Coconut Fish Curry	Popeye Frittata	Asian Pork Chops	Turkey with Spinach and Mushrooms	Parma Lemon Fish	Creamy Chili with Beef

WEEK 89	MONDAY	TUESDAY	WEDNESDAY	THURSDAY	FRIDAY	SATURDAY	SUNDAY
MEAL 1	Coconut Fish Curry	Japanese Balsamic Pork Roast	Hungarian beef goulash	Tuna Confit Salad	Champions Low-Carb Breakfast	Creamy Chili with Beef	Vegetarian Lasagna
MEAL 2	Sausage & Veggie Muffins	Mexican Pork Carnitas	Cauliflower and Broccoli Bake	Popeye Frittata	Citrus Creamy Fish	Cheesy Turkey with Mushrooms	Mexican Pork Carnitas
MEAL 3	Rotisserie Chicken	Tuscan Lamb Chops	Lemongrass braised chicken	Bacon-Stuffed Avocados	Worcestershire Chicken Salad	Sommerset Meatza	Sommerset Meatza

WEEK 90	MONDAY	TUESDAY	WEDNESDAY	THURSDAY	FRIDAY	SATURDAY	SUNDAY
MEAL 1	Sausage & Veggie Muffins	Champions Breakfast Hash	American Barbecue Turkey	British Lamb Ribs	Salmon with Asparagus	Smoked Salmon Avocado Stuffing	Spicy roasted chicken
MEAL 2	Rotisserie Chicken	Beef & Cheese Stuffed Peppers	Bacon-Stuffed Avocados	Smoked Salmon Avocado Stuffing	Mexican Pork Carnitas	American Barbecue Turkey	Tuscan Lamb Chops
MEAL 3	Beef & Cheese Stuffed Peppers	Tuscan Lamb Chops	British Lamb Ribs	Japanese Balsamic Pork Roast	Beef & Cheese Stuffed Peppers	Smoked Salmon Avocado Stuffing	Salmon with Asparagus

WEEK 91	MONDAY	TUESDAY	WEDNESDAY	THURSDAY	FRIDAY	SATURDAY	SUNDAY
MEAL 1	Champions Breakfast Hash	Salmon with Asparagus	Smoked Salmon Avocado Stuffing	Creamy Pasta	Sausage & Veggie Muffins	Lamb Chops in Masala Sauce	Citrus Creamy Fish
MEAL 2	Lamb Chops in Masala Sauce	Sausage & Veggie Muffins	Sommerset Meatza	American Barbecue Turkey	Turkey Meatballs	Bacon-Stuffed Avocados	Tuscan Lamb Chops
MEAL 3	Popeye Frittata	Beef-Stuffed Peppers	Creamy Pasta	Lemongrass braised chicken	Rotisserie Chicken	Japanese Balsamic Pork Roast	Sausage & Veggie Muffins

WEEK 92	MONDAY	TUESDAY	WEDNESDAY	THURSDAY	FRIDAY	SATURDAY	SUNDAY
MEAL 1	Salmon with Asparagus	Vegetarian Lasagna	Creamy Italian Chicken	Winter Lamb Stew	Japanese Balsamic Pork Roast	Turkey Meatballs	Spinach Mushroom Frittata
MEAL 2	Champions Low-Carb Breakfast	Asian Pork Chops	Smoked Salmon Avocado Stuffing	Hungarian beef goulash	Vegetarian Lasagna	Creamy Italian Chicken	Asian Pork Chops
MEAL 3	Turkey with Spinach and Mushrooms	Tuscan Lamb Chops	Hungarian beef goulash	Smoked Salmon Avocado Stuffing	Coconut Fish Curry	Coconut Fish Curry	Citrus Creamy Fish

WEEK 93	MONDAY	TUESDAY	WEDNESDAY	THURSDAY	FRIDAY	SATURDAY	SUNDAY
MEAL 1	Instant Carrot Chicken Pie	Vegetarian Lasagna	Parma Lemon Fish	Giant Pancake	Creamy Italian Chicken	Garlic Beef Steaks	Sweet & Sticky Chicken
MEAL 2	Spicy roasted chicken	Giant Pancake	Winter Lamb Stew	Champions Low-Carb Breakfast	Sausage & Veggie Muffins	Carrot & Potato Soup	Asian Pork Chops
MEAL 3	Japanese Balsamic Pork Roast	Instant Beef Steaks	British Lamb Ribs	Salmon with Asparagus	Ultimate Breakfast Platter	Instant Carrot Chicken Pie	Tuna Confit Salad

WEEK 94	MONDAY	TUESDAY	WEDNESDAY	THURSDAY	FRIDAY	SATURDAY	SUNDAY
MEAL 1	Beef meatballs in Marinara Sauce	Cottage Berry Pancake	Sausage & Veggie Muffins	Creamy Chili with Beef	Tijuana Chili Beef	Tijuana Chili Beef	Hungarian beef goulash
MEAL 2	Broccoli Soup	Garlic Beef Steaks	Giant Pancake	Instant Beef Steaks	Hungarian beef goulash	Spinach Mushroom Frittata	Vegetarian Lasagna
MEAL 3	Cheesy Turkey with Mushrooms	Rotisserie Chicken	Beef & Cheese Stuffed Peppers	Champions Breakfast Hash	Cottage Berry Pancake	Worcestershire Chicken Salad	Parma Lemon Fish

WEEK 95	MONDAY	TUESDAY	WEDNESDAY	THURSDAY	FRIDAY	SATURDAY	SUNDAY
MEAL 1	Carrot & Potato Soup	Mexican Pork Carnitas	Garlic Beef Steaks	Salmon with Asparagus	Tuscan Lamb Chops	Spicy roasted chicken	Tijuana Chili Beef
MEAL 2	Garlic Beef Steaks	Salmon with Asparagus	Beef & Cheese Stuffed Peppers	Sausage & Veggie Muffins	Champions Breakfast Hash	Champions Breakfast Hash	Hungarian beef goulash
MEAL 3	Beef-Stuffed Peppers	Vegetarian Lasagna	Turkey Meatballs	Beef-Stuffed Peppers	Creamy Italian Chicken	Turkey with Spinach and Mushrooms	Turkey Meatballs

WEEK 96	MONDAY	TUESDAY	WEDNESDAY	THURSDAY	FRIDAY	SATURDAY	SUNDAY
MEAL 1	Lemongrass braised chicken	Japanese Balsamic Pork Roast	Winter Lamb Stew	Vegetarian Lasagna	Coconut Fish Curry	Citrus Creamy Fish	Cheesy Turkey with Mushrooms
MEAL 2	Giant Pancake	Spinach Mushroom Frittata	Turkey with Spinach and Mushrooms	Asian Pork Chops	Sweet & Sticky Chicken	Salmon with Asparagus	Creamy Chili with Beef
MEAL 3	Hainanese Chicken	Turkey with Spinach and Mushrooms	Bacon-Stuffed Avocados	Tuscan Lamb Chops	Tuna Confit Salad	Sausage & Veggie Muffins	Giant Pancake

WEEK 97	MONDAY	TUESDAY	WEDNESDAY	THURSDAY	FRIDAY	SATURDAY	SUNDAY
MEAL 1	Lamb Chops in Masala Sauce	Portuguese Shanks	Tijuana Chili Beef	Creamy Pasta	Champions Breakfast Hash	Tuscan Lamb Chops	Salmon with Asparagus
MEAL 2	Spicy roasted chicken	Instant Carrot Chicken Pie	Parma Lemon Fish	Lemongrass braised chicken	Lamb Chops in Masala Sauce	Vegetarian Lasagna	Champions Low-Carb Breakfast
MEAL 3	Turkey with Spinach and Mushrooms	Garlic Beef Steaks	Smoked Salmon Avocado Stuffing	Instant Pizza	Popeye Frittata	Asian Pork Chops	Creamy Chili with Beef

WEEK 98	MONDAY	TUESDAY	WEDNESDAY	THURSDAY	FRIDAY	SATURDAY	SUNDAY
MEAL 1	Portobello Turkey legs	Creamy Pasta	Cheesy Turkey with Mushrooms	Garlic Beef Steaks	Salmon with Asparagus	Lebanese Zucchini Shakshuka	Instant Beef Steaks
MEAL 2	British Lamb Ribs	Spicy roasted chicken	Beef-Stuffed Peppers	Citrus Creamy Fish	Champions Low-Carb Breakfast	Beef meatballs in Marinara Sauce	Champions Breakfast Hash
MEAL 3	Winter Lamb Stew	Creamy Chili with Beef	Spicy roasted chicken	Beef meatballs in Marinara Sauce	Turkey with Spinach and Mushrooms	Portobello Turkey legs	Salmon with Asparagus

WEEK 99	MONDAY	TUESDAY	WEDNESDAY	THURSDAY	FRIDAY	SATURDAY	SUNDAY
MEAL 1	Broccoli Soup	Broccoli Soup	Parma Lemon Fish	Spicy roasted chicken	Instant Carrot Chicken Pie	Tilapia and shrimp paella	Sausage & Veggie Muffins
MEAL 2	Balsamic Turkey Meatballs	Creamy Pasta	Broccoli Soup	Carrot & Potato Soup	Spicy roasted chicken	Cauliflower and Broccoli Bake	Beef-Stuffed Peppers
MEAL 3	Tilapia and shrimp paella	Tijuana Chili Beef	Carrot & Potato Soup	Spicy roasted chicken	Japanese Balsamic Pork Roast	Popeye Frittata	Champions Breakfast Hash

WEEK 100	MONDAY	TUESDAY	WEDNESDAY	THURSDAY	FRIDAY	SATURDAY	SUNDAY
MEAL 1	Ultimate Breakfast Platter	Carrot & Potato Soup	Spicy roasted chicken	Broccoli Soup	Beef meatballs in Marinara Sauce	Hainanese Chicken	Garlic Beef Steaks
MEAL 2	Salmon with Asparagus	Spicy roasted chicken	Instant Pizza	Japanese Balsamic Pork Roast	Broccoli Soup	Hungarian beef goulash	Carrot & Potato Soup
MEAL 3	Instant Carrot Chicken Pie	Tuscan Lamb Chops	Sausage & Veggie Muffins	Broccoli Soup	Cheesy Turkey with Mushrooms	Cauliflower and Broccoli Bake	Instant Carrot Chicken Pie

WEEK 101	MONDAY	TUESDAY	WEDNESDAY	THURSDAY	FRIDAY	SATURDAY	SUNDAY
MEAL 1	Citrus Creamy Fish	Creamy Chicken Pie	Broccoli Soup	Parma Lemon Fish	Carrot & Potato Soup	Balsamic Turkey Meatballs	Tijuana Chili Beef
MEAL 2	Instant Pizza	Broccoli Soup	Cauliflower Chicken Rice	Cottage Berry Pancake	Garlic Beef Steaks	Lamb Chops in Masala Sauce	Spinach Mushroom Frittata
MEAL 3	Parma Lemon Fish	British Lamb Ribs	Giant Pancake	Creamy Chicken Pie	Beef-Stuffed Peppers	American Barbecue Turkey	Worcestershire Chicken Salad

WEEK 102	MONDAY	TUESDAY	WEDNESDAY	THURSDAY	FRIDAY	SATURDAY	SUNDAY
MEAL 1	Beef meatballs in Marinara Sauce	Carrot & Potato Soup	Sweet & Sticky Chicken	Worcestershire Chicken Salad	Lemongrass braised chicken	Smoked Salmon Avocado Stuffing	Spicy roasted chicken
MEAL 2	Sommerset Meatza	Spicy roasted chicken	British Lamb Ribs	Creamy Italian Chicken	Giant Pancake	American Barbecue Turkey	Tuscan Lamb Chops
MEAL 3	Creamy Chicken Pie	Worcestershire Chicken Salad	Spicy roasted chicken	Sweet & Sticky Chicken	Hainanese Chicken	Smoked Salmon Avocado Stuffing	Salmon with Asparagus

WEEK 103	MONDAY	TUESDAY	WEDNESDAY	THURSDAY	FRIDAY	SATURDAY	SUNDAY
MEAL 1	Worcestershire Chicken Salad	Portobello Turkey legs	Hainanese Chicken	Spicy roasted chicken	Lamb Chops in Masala Sauce	Lamb Chops in Masala Sauce	Citrus Creamy Fish
MEAL 2	British Lamb Ribs	Broccoli Soup	Turkey with Spinach and Mushrooms	Popeye Frittata	Spicy roasted chicken	Bacon-Stuffed Avocados	Tuscan Lamb Chops
MEAL 3	Popeye Frittata	Rotisserie Chicken	Broccoli Soup	Carrot & Potato Soup	Turkey with Spinach and Mushrooms	Japanese Balsamic Pork Roast	Sausage & Veggie Muffins

WEEK 104	MONDAY	TUESDAY	WEDNESDAY	THURSDAY	FRIDAY	SATURDAY	SUNDAY
MEAL 1	Portuguese Shanks	Hainanese Chicken	British Lamb Ribs	Lemongrass braised chicken	Portobello Turkey legs	Turkey Meatballs	Spinach Mushroom Frittata
MEAL 2	Creamy Chili with Beef	British Lamb Ribs	Cheesy Turkey with Mushrooms	Giant Pancake	British Lamb Ribs	Creamy Italian Chicken	Asian Pork Chops
MEAL 3	Creamy Italian Chicken	Carrot & Potato Soup	Lemongrass braised chicken	Broccoli Soup	Winter Lamb Stew	Coconut Fish Curry	Citrus Creamy Fish

WEEK 105	MONDAY	TUESDAY	WEDNESDAY	THURSDAY	FRIDAY	SATURDAY	SUNDAY
MEAL 1	Instant Beef Steaks	Balsamic Turkey Meatballs	Giant Pancake	Cauliflower Chicken Rice	Broccoli Soup	Japanese Balsamic Pork Roast	Champions Breakfast Hash
MEAL 2	Cheesy Turkey with Mushrooms	Instant Pizza	Instant Carrot Chicken Pie	Turkey Meatballs	Balsamic Turkey Meatballs	Vegetarian Lasagna	Turkey with Spinach and Mushrooms
MEAL 3	Spinach Mushroom Frittata	Japanese Balsamic Pork Roast	Mexican Pork Carnitas	Broccoli Soup	Tilapia and shrimp paella	Coconut Fish Curry	Popeye Frittata

WEEK 106	MONDAY	TUESDAY	WEDNESDAY	THURSDAY	FRIDAY	SATURDAY	SUNDAY
MEAL 1	Pork Roast in Honey and garlic	Spinach Mushroom Frittata	Instant Pizza	Lamb Chops in Masala Sauce	Ultimate Breakfast Platter	Japanese Balsamic Pork Roast	Hungarian beef goulash
MEAL 2	Portobello Turkey legs	Bacon-Stuffed Avocados	Broccoli Soup	Portobello Turkey legs	Salmon with Asparagus	Mexican Pork Carnitas	Cauliflower and Broccoli Bake
MEAL 3	Tilapia and shrimp paella	Instant Carrot Chicken Pie	Balsamic Turkey Meatballs	Instant Pizza	Instant Carrot Chicken Pie	Tuscan Lamb Chops	Lemongrass braised chicken

WEEK 107	MONDAY	TUESDAY	WEDNESDAY	THURSDAY	FRIDAY	SATURDAY	SUNDAY
MEAL 1	Portobello Turkey legs	Broccoli Soup	Spinach Mushroom Frittata	Bacon-Stuffed Avocados	Citrus Creamy Fish	Champions Breakfast Hash	American Barbecue Turkey
MEAL 2	Lamb Chops in Masala Sauce	Sweet & Sticky Chicken	Turkey Meatballs	British Lamb Ribs	Instant Pizza	Beef & Cheese Stuffed Peppers	Bacon-Stuffed Avocados
MEAL 3	Hungarian beef goulash	Cheesy Turkey with Mushrooms	Creamy Italian Chicken	Tuscan Lamb Chops	Parma Lemon Fish	Tuscan Lamb Chops	British Lamb Ribs

WEEK 108	MONDAY	TUESDAY	WEDNESDAY	THURSDAY	FRIDAY	SATURDAY	SUNDAY
MEAL 1	Tuna Confit Salad	Carrot & Potato Soup	Lemongrass braised chicken	Instant Pizza	Beef meatballs in Marinara Sauce	Salmon with Asparagus	Smoked Salmon Avocado Stuffing
MEAL 2	Balsamic Turkey Meatballs	British Lamb Ribs	Carrot & Potato Soup	Portuguese Shanks	Sommerset Meatza	Sausage & Veggie Muffins	Sommerset Meatza
MEAL 3	Popeye Frittata	Instant Pizza	Popeye Frittata	Carrot & Potato Soup	Creamy Chicken Pie	Beef-Stuffed Peppers	Creamy Pasta

WEEK 109	MONDAY	TUESDAY	WEDNESDAY	THURSDAY	FRIDAY	SATURDAY	SUNDAY
MEAL 1	Cauliflower and Broccoli Bake	Turkey Meatballs	Carrot & Potato Soup	Creamy Chicken Pie	Worcestershire Chicken Salad	Vegetarian Lasagna	Creamy Italian Chicken
MEAL 2	Hainanese Chicken	Hainanese Chicken	Creamy Chicken Pie	Creamy Italian Chicken	British Lamb Ribs	Asian Pork Chops	Smoked Salmon Avocado Stuffing
MEAL 3	Creamy Pasta	Creamy Chicken Pie	Bacon-Stuffed Avocados	Turkey with Spinach and Mushrooms	Popeye Frittata	Tuscan Lamb Chops	Hungarian beef goulash

WEEK 110	MONDAY	TUESDAY	WEDNESDAY	THURSDAY	FRIDAY	SATURDAY	SUNDAY
MEAL 1	Lemongrass braised chicken	Carrot & Potato Soup	Asian Pork Chops	Balsamic Turkey Meatballs	Portuguese Shanks	Vegetarian Lasagna	Parma Lemon Fish
MEAL 2	Smoked Salmon Avocado Stuffing	Asian Pork Chops	Carrot & Potato Soup	British Lamb Ribs	Creamy Chili with Beef	Giant Pancake	Winter Lamb Stew
MEAL 3	Sommerset Meatza	Spinach Mushroom Frittata	Coconut Fish Curry	Citrus Creamy Fish	Creamy Italian Chicken	Instant Beef Steaks	British Lamb Ribs

WEEK 111	MONDAY	TUESDAY	WEDNESDAY	THURSDAY	FRIDAY	SATURDAY	SUNDAY
MEAL 1	American Barbecue Turkey	Creamy Chicken Pie	Salmon with Asparagus	Rotisserie Chicken	Instant Beef Steaks	Cottage Berry Pancake	Sausage & Veggie Muffins
MEAL 2	Smoked Salmon Avocado Stuffing	Smoked Salmon Avocado Stuffing	Creamy Chicken Pie	Portobello Turkey legs	Cheesy Turkey with Mushrooms	Garlic Beef Steaks	Giant Pancake
MEAL 3	American Barbecue Turkey	Coconut Fish Curry	Worcestershire Chicken Salad	Creamy Chicken Pie	Spinach Mushroom Frittata	Rotisserie Chicken	Beef & Cheese Stuffed Peppers

WEEK 112	MONDAY	TUESDAY	WEDNESDAY	THURSDAY	FRIDAY	SATURDAY	SUNDAY
MEAL 1	Beef & Cheese Stuffed Peppers	Champions Low-Carb Breakfast	Spicy roasted chicken	Tilapia and shrimp paella	Creamy Chicken Pie	Mexican Pork Carnitas	Garlic Beef Steaks
MEAL 2	Coconut Fish Curry	Winter Lamb Stew	Sausage & Veggie Muffins	Creamy Chicken Pie	Asian Pork Chops	Salmon with Asparagus	Beef & Cheese Stuffed Peppers
MEAL 3	Winter Lamb Stew	Lemongrass braised chicken	Creamy Chicken Pie	Sausage & Veggie Muffins	Chili Chicken Rice	Vegetarian Lasagna	Turkey Meatballs

WEEK 113	MONDAY	TUESDAY	WEDNESDAY	THURSDAY	FRIDAY	SATURDAY	SUNDAY
MEAL 1	Turkey Meatballs	Tuscan Lamb Chops	Lamb Chops in Masala Sauce	Cheesy Turkey with Mushrooms	Creamy Italian Chicken	Japanese Balsamic Pork Roast	Winter Lamb Stew
MEAL 2	Creamy Italian Chicken	Parma Lemon Fish	Japanese Balsamic Pork Roast	Coconut Fish Curry	Beef-Stuffed Peppers	Spinach Mushroom Frittata	Turkey with Spinach and Mushrooms
MEAL 3	Japanese Balsamic Pork Roast	British Lamb Ribs	Smoked Salmon Avocado Stuffing	Cauliflower Chicken Rice	Tuscan Lamb Chops	Turkey with Spinach and Mushrooms	Bacon-Stuffed Avocados

WEEK 114	MONDAY	TUESDAY	WEDNESDAY	THURSDAY	FRIDAY	SATURDAY	SUNDAY
MEAL 1	Winter Lamb Stew	American Barbecue Turkey	Creamy Pasta	Mexican Pork Carnitas	Japanese Balsamic Pork Roast	Portuguese Shanks	Tijuana Chili Beef
MEAL 2	Beef & Cheese Stuffed Peppers	Instant Beef Steaks	Lemongrass braised chicken	Sausage & Veggie Muffins	Vegetarian Lasagna	Instant Carrot Chicken Pie	Parma Lemon Fish
MEAL 3	Salmon with Asparagus	Ultimate Breakfast Platter	Instant Pizza	Beef & Cheese Stuffed Peppers	Coconut Fish Curry	Garlic Beef Steaks	Smoked Salmon Avocado Stuffing

WEEK 115	MONDAY	TUESDAY	WEDNESDAY	THURSDAY	FRIDAY	SATURDAY	SUNDAY
MEAL 1	Beef & Cheese Stuffed Peppers	Instant Carrot Chicken Pie	Garlic Beef Steaks	Portobello Turkey legs	Spicy roasted chicken	Creamy Pasta	Cheesy Turkey with Mushrooms
MEAL 2	Mexican Pork Carnitas	Salmon with Asparagus	Citrus Creamy Fish	Sweet & Sticky Chicken	Instant Pizza	Spicy roasted chicken	Beef-Stuffed Peppers
MEAL 3	Sausage & Veggie Muffins	Creamy Chicken Pie	Beef meatballs in Marinara Sauce	Hainanese Chicken	Sausage & Veggie Muffins	Creamy Chili with Beef	Spicy roasted chicken

WEEK 116	MONDAY	TUESDAY	WEDNESDAY	THURSDAY	FRIDAY	SATURDAY	SUNDAY
MEAL 1	Rotisserie Chicken	Worcestershire Chicken Salad	Spicy roasted chicken	Tilapia and shrimp paella	Broccoli Soup	Broccoli Soup	Parma Lemon Fish
MEAL 2	Mexican Pork Carnitas	Spicy roasted chicken	Carrot & Potato Soup	Portuguese Shanks	Cauliflower Chicken Rice	Creamy Pasta	Broccoli Soup
MEAL 3	Spinach Mushroom Frittata	Sausage & Veggie Muffins	Spicy roasted chicken	Spinach Mushroom Frittata	Giant Pancake	Tijuana Chili Beef	Carrot & Potato Soup

WEEK 117	MONDAY	TUESDAY	WEDNESDAY	THURSDAY	FRIDAY	SATURDAY	SUNDAY
MEAL 1	Tijuana Chili Beef	Creamy Chicken Pie	Broccoli Soup	British Lamb Ribs	Sweet & Sticky Chicken	Carrot & Potato Soup	Spicy roasted chicken
MEAL 2	Turkey with Spinach and Mushrooms	Vegetarian Lasagna	Japanese Balsamic Pork Roast	Japanese Balsamic Pork Roast	British Lamb Ribs	Spicy roasted chicken	Instant Pizza
MEAL 3	Sweet & Sticky Chicken	Lamb Chops in Masala Sauce	Broccoli Soup	Ultimate Breakfast Platter	Spicy roasted chicken	Tuscan Lamb Chops	Sausage & Veggie Muffins

WEEK 118	MONDAY	TUESDAY	WEDNESDAY	THURSDAY	FRIDAY	SATURDAY	SUNDAY
MEAL 1	Tuna Confit Salad	Japanese Balsamic Pork Roast	Parma Lemon Fish	Salmon with Asparagus	Hainanese Chicken	Spicy roasted chicken	Smoked Salmon Avocado Stuffing
MEAL 2	Asian Pork Chops	Smoked Salmon Avocado Stuffing	Cottage Berry Pancake	American Barbecue Turkey	Turkey with Spinach and Mushrooms	Popeye Frittata	Sommerset Meatza
MEAL 3	Hungarian beef goulash	Tuscan Lamb Chops	Creamy Chicken Pie	Broccoli Soup	Broccoli Soup	Carrot & Potato Soup	Creamy Pasta

WEEK 119	MONDAY	TUESDAY	WEDNESDAY	THURSDAY	FRIDAY	SATURDAY	SUNDAY
MEAL 1	Creamy Chicken Pie	Cauliflower Chicken Rice	Worcestershire Chicken Salad	Smoked Salmon Avocado Stuffing	British Lamb Ribs	Lemongrass braised chicken	Creamy Chicken Pie
MEAL 2	Japanese Balsamic Pork Roast	Rotisserie Chicken	Creamy Italian Chicken	American Barbecue Turkey	Cheesy Turkey with Mushrooms	Giant Pancake	Creamy Chili with Beef
MEAL 3	Tuna Confit Salad	Tilapia and shrimp paella	Sweet & Sticky Chicken	Broccoli Soup	Lemongrass braised chicken	Broccoli Soup	Vegetarian Lasagna

WEEK 120	MONDAY	TUESDAY	WEDNESDAY	THURSDAY	FRIDAY	SATURDAY	SUNDAY
MEAL 1	Lebanese Zucchini Shakshuka	Tilapia and shrimp paella	Spicy roasted chicken	Beef & Cheese Stuffed Peppers	Giant Pancake	Cauliflower Chicken Rice	Beef-Stuffed Peppers
MEAL 2	Beef meatballs in Marinara Sauce	Creamy Chicken Pie	Popeye Frittata	Coconut Fish Curry	Instant Carrot Chicken Pie	Turkey Meatballs	Tilapia and shrimp paella
MEAL 3	Lebanese Zucchini Shakshuka	Coconut Fish Curry	Carrot & Potato Soup	Winter Lamb Stew	Mexican Pork Carnitas	Broccoli Soup	Creamy Chicken Pie

WEEK 121	MONDAY	TUESDAY	WEDNESDAY	THURSDAY	FRIDAY	SATURDAY	SUNDAY
MEAL 1	Tilapia and shrimp paella	Instant Beef Steaks	Lemongrass braised chicken	Broccoli Soup	Instant Pizza	Lamb Chops in Masala Sauce	Coconut Fish Curry
MEAL 2	Lebanese Zucchini Shakshuka	Chili Chicken Rice	Giant Pancake	Turkey Meatballs	Broccoli Soup	Portobello Turkey legs	Instant Beef Steaks
MEAL 3	Spicy roasted chicken	Spicy roasted chicken	Broccoli Soup	Creamy Italian Chicken	Balsamic Turkey Meatballs	Instant Pizza	Lemongrass braised chicken

WEEK 122	MONDAY	TUESDAY	WEDNESDAY	THURSDAY	FRIDAY	SATURDAY	SUNDAY
MEAL 1	Beef meatballs in Marinara Sauce	Lemongrass braised chicken	Cauliflower Chicken Rice	Japanese Balsamic Pork Roast	Spinach Mushroom Frittata	Bacon-Stuffed Avocados	Chili Chicken Rice
MEAL 2	Balsamic Turkey Meatballs	Broccoli Soup	Turkey Meatballs	Cauliflower Chicken Rice	Turkey Meatballs	British Lamb Ribs	Champions Low-Carb Breakfast
MEAL 3	Hainanese Chicken	Beef & Cheese Stuffed Peppers	Broccoli Soup	Winter Lamb Stew	Creamy Italian Chicken	Tuscan Lamb Chops	Beef-Stuffed Peppers

WEEK 123	MONDAY	TUESDAY	WEDNESDAY	THURSDAY	FRIDAY	SATURDAY	SUNDAY
MEAL 1	Balsamic Turkey Meatballs	Spinach Mushroom Frittata	Lamb Chops in Masala Sauce	Beef & Cheese Stuffed Peppers	Lemongrass braised chicken	Instant Pizza	Instant Pizza
MEAL 2	Cauliflower and Broccoli Bake	Creamy Chicken Pie	Portobello Turkey legs	Salmon with Asparagus	Carrot & Potato Soup	Portuguese Shanks	Cottage Berry Pancake
MEAL 3	Hungarian beef goulash	Parma Lemon Fish	Instant Pizza	Cauliflower Chicken Rice	Popeye Frittata	Carrot & Potato Soup	Parma Lemon Fish

WEEK 124	MONDAY	TUESDAY	WEDNESDAY	THURSDAY	FRIDAY	SATURDAY	SUNDAY
MEAL 1	Tuna Confit Salad	Smoked Salmon Avocado Stuffing	Bacon-Stuffed Avocados	Beef & Cheese Stuffed Peppers	Carrot & Potato Soup	Creamy Chicken Pie	Beef-Stuffed Peppers
MEAL 2	Popeye Frittata	Sommerset Meatza	British Lamb Ribs	Mexican Pork Carnitas	Creamy Chicken Pie	Creamy Italian Chicken	Garlic Beef Steaks
MEAL 3	Bacon-Stuffed Avocados	Creamy Pasta	Tuscan Lamb Chops	Sausage & Veggie Muffins	Bacon-Stuffed Avocados	Turkey with Spinach and Mushrooms	Carrot & Potato Soup

WEEK 125	MONDAY	TUESDAY	WEDNESDAY	THURSDAY	FRIDAY	SATURDAY	SUNDAY
MEAL 1	British Lamb Ribs	Creamy Italian Chicken	Instant Pizza	Cauliflower Chicken Rice	Asian Pork Chops	Balsamic Turkey Meatballs	Instant Carrot Chicken Pie
MEAL 2	Smoked Salmon Avocado Stuffing	Turkey Meatballs	Portuguese Shanks	Rotisserie Chicken	Carrot & Potato Soup	British Lamb Ribs	Beef-Stuffed Peppers
MEAL 3	Japanese Balsamic Pork Roast	Japanese Balsamic Pork Roast	Carrot & Potato Soup	Mexican Pork Carnitas	Coconut Fish Curry	Citrus Creamy Fish	Broccoli Soup

WEEK 126	MONDAY	TUESDAY	WEDNESDAY	THURSDAY	FRIDAY	SATURDAY	SUNDAY
MEAL 1	Creamy Pasta	Winter Lamb Stew	Creamy Chicken Pie	Spinach Mushroom Frittata	Salmon with Asparagus	Rotisserie Chicken	Tijuana Chili Beef
MEAL 2	American Barbecue Turkey	Salmon with Asparagus	Creamy Italian Chicken	Creamy Chili with Beef	Creamy Chicken Pie	Portobello Turkey legs	Spinach Mushroom Frittata
MEAL 3	Lemongrass braised chicken	Worcestershire Chicken Salad	Turkey with Spinach and Mushrooms	British Lamb Ribs	Worcestershire Chicken Salad	Creamy Chicken Pie	Beef-Stuffed Peppers

WEEK 127	MONDAY	TUESDAY	WEDNESDAY	THURSDAY	FRIDAY	SATURDAY	SUNDAY
MEAL 1	Winter Lamb Stew	Spicy roasted chicken	Balsamic Turkey Meatballs	Japanese Balsamic Pork Roast	Spicy roasted chicken	Tilapia and shrimp paella	Worcestershire Chicken Salad
MEAL 2	Japanese Balsamic Pork Roast	Carrot & Potato Soup	British Lamb Ribs	Vegetarian Lasagna	Sausage & Veggie Muffins	Creamy Chicken Pie	Champions Breakfast Hash
MEAL 3	Turkey Meatballs	Turkey with Spinach and Mushrooms	Citrus Creamy Fish	Coconut Fish Curry	Creamy Chicken Pie	Sausage & Veggie Muffins	Spicy roasted chicken

WEEK 128	MONDAY	TUESDAY	WEDNESDAY	THURSDAY	FRIDAY	SATURDAY	SUNDAY
MEAL 1	Creamy Italian Chicken	Broccoli Soup	Rotisserie Chicken	Tilapia and shrimp paella	Lamb Chops in Masala Sauce	Cheesy Turkey with Mushrooms	Beef-Stuffed Peppers
MEAL 2	Winter Lamb Stew	Spicy roasted chicken	Portobello Turkey legs	Creamy Chicken Pie	Japanese Balsamic Pork Roast	Coconut Fish Curry	Lemongrass braised chicken
MEAL 3	Creamy Italian Chicken	Creamy Italian Chicken	Creamy Chicken Pie	Sausage & Veggie Muffins	Smoked Salmon Avocado Stuffing	Cauliflower Chicken Rice	Broccoli Soup

WEEK 129	MONDAY	TUESDAY	WEDNESDAY	THURSDAY	FRIDAY	SATURDAY	SUNDAY
MEAL 1	American Barbecue Turkey	Sausage & Veggie Muffins	Tilapia and shrimp paella	Smoked Salmon Avocado Stuffing	Tuscan Lamb Chops	Japanese Balsamic Pork Roast	Beef & Cheese Stuffed Peppers
MEAL 2	Spinach Mushroom Frittata	Salmon with Asparagus	Creamy Chicken Pie	Sommerset Meatza	Cauliflower Chicken Rice	Beef meatballs in Marinara Sauce	Giant Pancake
MEAL 3	Hungarian beef goulash	Carrot & Potato Soup	Sausage & Veggie Muffins	Creamy Pasta	Rotisserie Chicken	Hainanese Chicken	Instant Carrot Chicken Pie

WEEK 130	MONDAY	TUESDAY	WEDNESDAY	THURSDAY	FRIDAY	SATURDAY	SUNDAY
MEAL 1	Beef meatballs in Marinara Sauce	Coconut Fish Curry	Cheesy Turkey with Mushrooms	Beef meatballs in Marinara Sauce	American Barbecue Turkey	Creamy Italian Chicken	Mexican Pork Carnitas
MEAL 2	Lebanese Zucchini Shakshuka	Spinach Mushroom Frittata	Coconut Fish Curry	Lebanese Zucchini Shakshuka	Smoked Salmon Avocado Stuffing	Turkey Meatballs	Instant Pizza
MEAL 3	Tilapia and shrimp paella	Chili Chicken Rice	Cauliflower Chicken Rice	Tilapia and shrimp paella	American Barbecue Turkey	Japanese Balsamic Pork Roast	Broccoli Soup

WEEK 131	MONDAY	TUESDAY	WEDNESDAY	THURSDAY	FRIDAY	SATURDAY	SUNDAY
MEAL 1	Beef meatballs in Marinara Sauce	Turkey Meatballs	Japanese Balsamic Pork Roast	Spicy roasted chicken	Beef & Cheese Stuffed Peppers	Japanese Balsamic Pork Roast	Balsamic Turkey Meatballs
MEAL 2	Portuguese Shanks	British Lamb Ribs	Beef meatballs in Marinara Sauce	Popeye Frittata	Coconut Fish Curry	Ultimate Breakfast Platter	Cauliflower Chicken Rice
MEAL 3	Pork Roast in Honey and garlic	Spinach Mushroom Frittata	Hainanese Chicken	Carrot & Potato Soup	Winter Lamb Stew	Salmon with Asparagus	Citrus Creamy Fish

WEEK 132	MONDAY	TUESDAY	WEDNESDAY	THURSDAY	FRIDAY	SATURDAY	SUNDAY
MEAL 1	Portuguese Shanks	Smoked Salmon Avocado Stuffing	Asian Pork Chops	Vegetarian Lasagna	Turkey Meatballs	Coconut Fish Curry	Spinach Mushroom Frittata
MEAL 2	Popeye Frittata	Lemongrass braised chicken	Creamy Chili with Beef	Giant Pancake	Creamy Italian Chicken	Turkey with Spinach and Mushrooms	Coconut Fish Curry
MEAL 3	Lamb Chops in Masala Sauce	Sausage & Veggie Muffins	British Lamb Ribs	Instant Beef Steaks	Japanese Balsamic Pork Roast	Creamy Chicken Pie	Creamy Chicken Pie

WEEK 133	MONDAY	TUESDAY	WEDNESDAY	THURSDAY	FRIDAY	SATURDAY	SUNDAY
MEAL 1	Cauliflower and Broccoli Bake	Chili Chicken Rice	Vegetarian Lasagna	Cottage Berry Pancake	Winter Lamb Stew	Chili Chicken Rice	Smoked Salmon Avocado Stuffing
MEAL 2	Tuna Confit Salad	British Lamb Ribs	Creamy Chicken Pie	Garlic Beef Steaks	Beef & Cheese Stuffed Peppers	Beef meatballs in Marinara Sauce	Coconut Fish Curry
MEAL 3	Lamb Chops in Masala Sauce	Salmon with Asparagus	Spicy roasted chicken	Rotisserie Chicken	Salmon with Asparagus	Asian Pork Chops	Coconut Fish Curry

WEEK 134	MONDAY	TUESDAY	WEDNESDAY	THURSDAY	FRIDAY	SATURDAY	SUNDAY
MEAL 1	Popeye Frittata	Champions Low-Carb Breakfast	Instant Carrot Chicken Pie	American Barbecue Turkey	Beef & Cheese Stuffed Peppers	Creamy Italian Chicken	Champions Low-Carb Breakfast
MEAL 2	Balsamic Turkey Meatballs	Creamy Chicken Pie	Winter Lamb Stew	Sausage & Veggie Muffins	Mexican Pork Carnitas	Balsamic Turkey Meatballs	Winter Lamb Stew
MEAL 3	British Lamb Ribs	Chili Chicken Rice	Hungarian beef goulash	Cheesy Turkey with Mushrooms	Sausage & Veggie Muffins	Vegetarian Lasagna	Lemongrass braised chicken

WEEK 135	MONDAY	TUESDAY	WEDNESDAY	THURSDAY	FRIDAY	SATURDAY	SUNDAY
MEAL 1	Bacon-Stuffed Avocados	Citrus Creamy Fish	Ultimate Breakfast Platter	Citrus Creamy Fish	Rotisserie Chicken	Lemongrass braised chicken	Champions Breakfast Hash
MEAL 2	Lemongrass braised chicken	Creamy Chicken Pie	Sommerset Meatza	Cauliflower and Broccoli Bake	Mexican Pork Carnitas	Hungarian beef goulash	Tuscan Lamb Chops
MEAL 3	Creamy Pasta	Sommerset Meatza	Champions Low-Carb Breakfast	Tuscan Lamb Chops	Spinach Mushroom Frittata	Spicy roasted chicken	Parma Lemon Fish

WEEK 136	MONDAY	TUESDAY	WEDNESDAY	THURSDAY	FRIDAY	SATURDAY	SUNDAY
MEAL 1	Sommerset Meatza	Asian Pork Chops	Parma Lemon Fish	Portobello Turkey legs	Beef & Cheese Stuffed Peppers	Portuguese Shanks	British Lamb Ribs
MEAL 2	Lemongrass braised chicken	Turkey with Spinach and Mushrooms	Sweet & Sticky Chicken	Sommerset Meatza	Coconut Fish Curry	Winter Lamb Stew	Beef & Cheese Stuffed Peppers
MEAL 3	British Lamb Ribs	Portuguese Shanks	Beef-Stuffed Peppers	Champions Low-Carb Breakfast	Winter Lamb Stew	Popeye Frittata	Winter Lamb Stew

WEEK 137	MONDAY	TUESDAY	WEDNESDAY	THURSDAY	FRIDAY	SATURDAY	SUNDAY
MEAL 1	Coconut Fish Curry	Mexican Pork Carnitas	Asian Pork Chops	Tilapia and shrimp paella	Turkey Meatballs	Portuguese Shanks	Hungarian beef goulash
MEAL 2	Winter Lamb Stew	Citrus Creamy Fish	Smoked Salmon Avocado Stuffing	Sweet & Sticky Chicken	Creamy Italian Chicken	Sausage & Veggie Muffins	Cauliflower Chicken Rice
MEAL 3	Creamy Italian Chicken	Creamy Chili with Beef	Instant Beef Steaks	Hainanese Chicken	Japanese Balsamic Pork Roast	Hainanese Chicken	Citrus Creamy Fish

WEEK 138	MONDAY	TUESDAY	WEDNESDAY	THURSDAY	FRIDAY	SATURDAY	SUNDAY
MEAL 1	Vegetarian Lasagna	Cottage Berry Pancake	Beef & Cheese Stuffed Peppers	Parma Lemon Fish	Winter Lamb Stew	Spicy roasted chicken	Creamy Chicken Pie
MEAL 2	Turkey Meatballs	Portobello Turkey legs	Coconut Fish Curry	Cottage Berry Pancake	Beef & Cheese Stuffed Peppers	Popeye Frittata	Turkey with Spinach and Mushrooms
MEAL 3	Vegetarian Lasagna	Popeye Frittata	Winter Lamb Stew	Creamy Chicken Pie	Salmon with Asparagus	Tuna Confit Salad	Turkey Meatballs

WEEK 139	MONDAY	TUESDAY	WEDNESDAY	THURSDAY	FRIDAY	SATURDAY	SUNDAY
MEAL 1	Beef-Stuffed Peppers	Lamb Chops in Masala Sauce	Turkey Meatballs	Worcestershire Chicken Salad	American Barbecue Turkey	Rotisserie Chicken	Popeye Frittata
MEAL 2	Tuscan Lamb Chops	Tilapia and shrimp paella	Creamy Italian Chicken	Creamy Italian Chicken	Bacon-Stuffed Avocados	Broccoli Soup	Tuna Confit Salad
MEAL 3	Mexican Pork Carnitas	Sommerset Meatza	Japanese Balsamic Pork Roast	Sweet & Sticky Chicken	British Lamb Ribs	Spinach Mushroom Frittata	Sausage & Veggie Muffins

WEEK 140	MONDAY	TUESDAY	WEDNESDAY	THURSDAY	FRIDAY	SATURDAY	SUNDAY
MEAL 1	Salmon with Asparagus	Champions Breakfast Hash	Winter Lamb Stew	Beef meatballs in Marinara Sauce	Smoked Salmon Avocado Stuffing	Instant Carrot Chicken Pie	Salmon with Asparagus
MEAL 2	Sausage & Veggie Muffins	Asian Pork Chops	Beef & Cheese Stuffed Peppers	Broccoli Soup	Sommerset Meatza	Creamy Italian Chicken	Lamb Chops in Masala Sauce
MEAL 3	Rotisserie Chicken	British Lamb Ribs	Salmon with Asparagus	Cheesy Turkey with Mushrooms	Creamy Pasta	Creamy Pasta	Winter Lamb Stew

Printed in Great Britain
by Amazon

35912116R00066